The really useful guide to
Kings and Queens of England

Historic
Royal Palaces

Contents

What does it take to make a monarch?

The climax of the coronation ceremony, the moment of crowning, captured in *The Coronation of Queen Victoria* by Edmund Thomas Paris, 1838 (detail)

'The king is dead, long live the king!' That is what they say at a monarch's death, to preserve the appearance of continuity. The line back to William the Conqueror, who won the English crown in 1066, has had only one serious break in the republican experiment of 1649-60. Otherwise, there has been one line based on the hereditary principle. Queen Elizabeth II can trace her ancestry back to the Conqueror, and before. But the line has bent and buckled many times in the course of a thousand years.

A sovereign is usually a man. Inheritance favours males. The first woman on the throne came once internal peace was better established; a monarch was no longer expected to lead an army personally. The female line has preserved the continuity – the transition from Queen Anne to King George I in 1714 was because his great-great-grandfather was James I, he was closest in line and a Protestant.

Religion caused as much royal and national strife since the 16th century as dynastic struggles caused in the preceding three centuries. The official national religion is – essentially – the monarch's religion. A monarch swears to uphold the rights of he Church ahead of any others at the coronation.

Being crowned is another defining aspect of monarchy. Crown, orb and sceptre are symbols of royal power, and almost every monarch has gone through the ceremony. Edward VIII, who reigned briefly in 1936, is known to posterity as the uncrowned king.

Monarchs rule at the will of the people and under the law. Tendencies towards absolute or despotic power have always been curtailed. Monarchs have been supported – and superseded – by parliaments for almost eight centuries. Rights and privileges enshrined in Magna Carta have been re-stated many times over the years.

English monarchs are also usually something else. The Conqueror was Norman, and many medieval kings were more French than they were English. In 1603, with the union of the crowns, Scots held the English throne. In 1714, the British throne was held by Germans, and the strength of the German connection has been the greatest single influence ever since.

Here they follow, in sequence, the kings and queens of England in all their glory and shame.

Edward the Confessor 1042-66

Renowned as a gentle, saintly king; in reality a tough political survivor

Useful factfile

Born Between 1003 and 1005 at Islip, near Oxford

Crowned 3 April (Easter Day) 1043 at Winchester

Died 4 or 5 January 1066, aged about 61, at the Palace of Westminster. Buried Westminster Abbey

Parents King Æthelred II of England and Queen Emma, sister of the Duke of Normandy

Married Edith, daughter of Earl Godwine of Wessex, 1045

Children None

Canonised Papal bull issued on 7 February 1161.

Greatest victory Edward was the seventh son of King Æthelred II, and eventually came to the throne having outlived and outsmarted all other contenders.

Greatest virtue Edward and Edith's marriage was childless, a fact seized on and celebrated by celibate monks after his death. These admiring holy biographers claimed that the pious 'Saint' King Edward and his wife had refrained from sex.

> ʿHe loved, but was not weakened; she was beloved, but untouchedʾ
>
> Ælred of Rievaulx, Edward's biographer, writing of Edward and Edith's alleged chastity.

Special powers Ælred of Rievaulx writes about a miracle performed by Edward when a woman afflicted with tumours on her neck begged for his help. Undaunted, the King washed and made the sign of the cross over them. 'At once the skin broke, worms gushed out with the infection, the swelling subsided, the pain disappeared.' From the 13th century, the ritual of 'Touching for the King's Evil', whereby the monarch dispels the disease of scrofula from their unfortunate subjects, became a tradition of some five hundred years standing. It continued until the accession of George I in 1714.

Legacy Edward's childlessness ushered in the Norman Conquest. The story of Edward making 'William the Bastard' of Normandy his heir, and thus legitimising the Duke's invasion of England, is famously sewn into the Bayeux Tapestry.

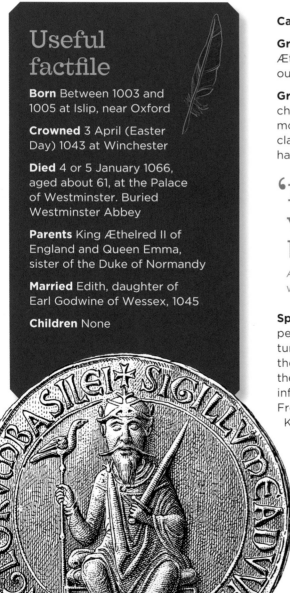

The seal of Edward the Confessor

What kind of ruler?

Edward came to the throne after years of exile in Normandy. He had to endure a domineering mother and, after he married, a ruthless and ambitious father-in-law, Earl Godwine of Wessex. Edward and his wife Edith had no children, so although Edward ruled wisely and well and united a fragmented kingdom, his lack of an heir plunged the country into turmoil upon his death. Edward built the first Westminster Abbey, and after his death became known for his piety (hence his descriptive name 'Confessor'). A century later, he was canonised, and became known as Saint Edward the Confessor.

King Edward and courtiers shown in a detail from the Bayeux Tapestry

A richly embellished 15th-century manuscript showing King Edward at a royal banquet

Anglo-Saxons

Harold II 1066

A fine warrior and the richest man in England, but took an arrow in the eye at the Battle of Hastings, allegedly

Harold II's coronation recorded in the Bayeux Tapestry (detail)

What kind of ruler?

Harold was named as king by a dying Edward the Confessor, although he had no hereditary claim to the throne. He was soon threatened with marauding raids and an ever-present threat of invasion, first from the Norwegians, whom he defeated at Stamford Bridge in Yorkshire, only to learn that the Normans had landed in Sussex. The exhausted English army headed south to fight William of Normandy's men at the famous Battle of Hastings. Harold's heroic end, traditionally by arrow but perhaps actually hacked to death, and the defeat of the English, cleared the way for the Conqueror and the domination of the Normans.

The crowned head of Harold II on a silver penny

Useful factfile

Born c1023

Crowned 6 January 1066, the first king crowned in Westminster Abbey

Died 14 October 1066, aged 44. Buried Battle, East Sussex, later Waltham Abbey, Essex

Parents Godwine, Earl of Wessex and Gytha

Married 1 Edyth Swan-neck, c1045 in a Danish 'handfast' union; 2 Ealdgyth of Mercia, c1065

Children six by Edyth Swan-neck and a son, Harold Haroldson, by Ealdgyth

Hearing that the gigantic Viking King Harald Hardrada was after his land, Harold grimly offered him

'six feet of English soil or as much more as he is taller than other men'

Likes Angles and Saxons.

Dislikes Normans and Norsemen.

Weird claim to fame Often called 'The last English King', in fact his mother was Danish. He was the last King of England not of royal blood.

Physical oddity We don't know, but his body was identified by Edyth Swan-neck after his death by certain private marks known only to her.

Greatest victory Stamford Bridge 1066, over the Norwegian ruler Harald Hardrada.

Greatest defeat The Battle of Hastings, 1066. The most famous date in English history. Harold, two of his brothers and the leading English warriors died fighting to the last.

Finest hour Standing with his household warriors on the ridge of Senlac Hill at Battle, East Sussex, under the banners of the Dragon and the Fighting Man of Wessex, to hold back the Norman invaders. The English shouted 'Out! Out! Out!' as the invincible Norman cavalry charged up to meet them.

Worst mistake Somehow ending up in the court of his rival, Duke William of Normandy. He allowed the Normans to portray him as a liar and usurper.

Royal mystery Did he promise the crown to William of Normandy, only to go back on his word?

Royal scandal Later more prudish ages classed Edyth Swan-neck as Harold's mistress. To contemporaries, they had a 'Danish marriage', not sanctioned by the Church.

Unhappy end Supposedly killed by an arrow in his eye at Hastings. His body was viciously mutilated by the Normans.

The Normans

William I
1066-87

Big, short-haired Norman Conqueror (and Bastard)

Useful factfile

Born *c*1027 or 1028, Falais, Normandy

Crowned Christmas Day 1066, Westminster Abbey

Died 9 September 1087, aged about 59, in St Gervais, France. Buried Abbey of St Stephen, Caen

Parents Duke Robert 'the Devil' of Normandy and Herlève, allegedly a tanner's daughter from Falais

Married Matilda of Flanders, 1053

Children Four sons: Robert Duke of Normandy, Richard, William Rufus (later William II) and Henry (later Henry I); five daughters including Adéla, Countess of Blois

Also known as 'The Bastard' (before 1066), 'The Conqueror' (after 1066).

Claim to fame The ancestor of all the subsequent kings and queens of England, Great Britain and the United Kingdom, who held the throne ultimately by right of his conquest.

Physical oddity William was tall and became quite fat. His wife Matilda's skeleton showed she was only four feet tall. As far as we know no-one commented on this at the time.

Greatest victory The Battle of Hastings, 1066, victory over King Harold of England. William went on to conquer the whole kingdom.

Biggest misunderstanding At William's coronation the shouts of the congregation accepting William as king alarmed the Norman guards outside. Fearing insurrection, they set fire to some of the nearby buildings. Most people took flight, but a few terrified clergy remained to complete the consecration of the visibly shaking King. This is said to be the only time William ever showed fear.

Literary achievement William's officers travelled his new won kingdom to record the owner of every piece of land and (according to a shocked English writer) 'shameful to relate, every ox or cow or pig'. Not used to such prying into their personal affairs, the English felt they were being called up before God at the end of the world. The resulting huge survey, 'like the judgement of God, with which there is no discussion' was therefore to be known as *Domesday Book*.

A silver coin bearing the image of William I

Artistic style Norman. His half-brother, Bishop Odo of Bayeux, figures prominently in the Bayeux tapestry, recording the Norman invasion, and probably commissioned it. William favoured the use of the distinct light-golden coloured stone from Caen in Normandy. Caen stone became the stone of choice for Norman buildings such as the White Tower in preference to native English varieties.

Unhappy end In conquering style, William died sacking the City of Nantes. He fell from his horse, overcome by heat or injured by being thrown against his saddle pommel.

What kind of ruler?

Ruthless. A hard man in every way: a vicious warrior, a harsh ruler, a driving administrator. His temper was fearsome, and his suppression was cruel, but he changed the shape of England, with a tax system, a programme of land tenure and military organisation. The meticulous Domesday survey was a great achievement.

Portrait of William I by an unknown artist, c1620

A 14th-century manuscript of the Conqueror, resplendent in full military regalia

Palace connections

Started building the **White Tower**, at the centre of today's **Tower of London**

Palace connections:
The Tower of London

The Tower has always been not only a most useful fortress for the monarchy and institutions of State, but also an architectural symbol of royal majesty and might

William the Conqueror began the process by ordering the construction of the great stone keep – later known as the White Tower – in the south eastern corner of the ancient Roman city walls. His son **William Rufus** completed the job, and England's newest dynasty had a magnificent and impressive fortress/palace, complete with an exquisite royal chapel, in which to conduct their daily life on the rare occasions that royalty chose to stay. The castle was expanded westwards in the 12th century by the officers of **Richard I** or his brother **John**. John is the first recorded monarch to have kept lions at the Tower – a tradition that continued up until 1832. Subsequent

kings and queens expanded the Tower's royal menagerie, conveniently depositing exotic beasts received as diplomatic gifts. **Henry III**, who exploited the Tower as both a place of refuge in times of trouble and as a weapon to intimidate rebellious subjects, enlarged the fortress still further. He protected the castle with a curtain wall defended by mural towers, and in 1240 ordered the great keep to be painted white – to make it look even more impressive. New lodgings were built to house Henry's family, and the Tower's chapels were filled with paintings, sculptures and stained glass.

William the Conqueror from the Bayeux Tapestry (detail)

The Norman White Tower at the heart of the fortress, with Henry VIII's ogee-shaped turrets

Henry's son, **Edward I**, turned the Tower into a 'concentric' castle, by encircling his father's work with another heavily defended curtain wall. War-like Edward focussed on the fortress' defences, and reclaimed land from the River Thames, creating the Outer Ward, and excavated a sluiced water-filled moat, to prevent undermining by attackers. He began the construction of the wharf, and built a new fortified land entrance to the castle. Edward also had magnificent new lodgings built for himself overlooking the river, complete with a chapel, expensively tiled floors, and painted external sculptures. Like most monarchs, he would have arrived at the Tower by river, and his lodgings were built over a huge arched watergate, which in later centuries became notorious as Traitors' Gate. Although subsequent monarchs built at the Tower, the shape of the castle as it was at the end of Edward's reign is more or less the one we have inherited. Only fragments survive from the building campaigns of later medieval monarchs, and just two complete buildings from Henry VIII's tumultuous reign. The silhouette of the White Tower is dominated today by the ogee-shaped

roofs **Henry VIII** added to the turrets as part of his flamboyant preparations for Anne Boleyn's coronation procession. This began at the Tower on the day before the coronation and ended at Westminster, as it had for all kings and queens since the late middle ages. **Charles II** was the last monarch to observe the tradition in 1660.

The buildings of the Tower today reflect the 19th-century's fascination with medieval architecture – **Queen Victoria's** consort Prince Albert encouraged the restoration of the castle. New battlements were added, old buildings were demolished or re-faced in stone if too decrepit or not 'gothic' enough, and those imprisoned or executed within the Tower's walls were commemorated with plaques. Former prisons inscribed with religious graffiti were opened to the public, and romantic legends grew up about the fall of the British monarchy, should the Tower Ravens ever leave. To date there are six ravens in residence, and the monarchy appears to be here to stay...

William II
1087-1100

Red faced, foul-mouthed, blaspheming bachelor, shot in mysterious circumstances while hunting

Useful factfile

Born 1060, Normandy

Crowned 26 September 1087, Westminster Abbey

Died 2 August 1100, aged about 40, in the New Forest. Buried Winchester Cathedral

Parents William the Conqueror and Matilda of Flanders

Married Never

Children None

Palace connections

William finished his father's White Tower at the **Tower of London**

Claim to fame The only adult king of England never to marry.

Physical oddity William went bright red in the face, from anger, drinking or over-indulgence. Hence his nickname 'Rufus' (the Red).

Greatest achievement The White Tower. William also built Westminster Great Hall, the largest enclosed secular space in Europe, which remains at the heart of government.

Finest hour A bold and chivalrous knight, William was bequeathed England by his father, and rushed to claim the throne ahead of his eldest brother, who had to make do with the Duchy of Normandy.

Royal scandal Shocked conservative churchmen by mocking the Christian religion, and by frequent use of blasphemous and suggestive oaths.

Personal style Always dressed in the height of fashion, considered outrageous by the Church. He wore his hair long with a bare forehead. His tunics were cut very short and worse, he wore expensive shoes with long points curled up 'like scorpions' tails'. He berated a shoemaker who brought him a relatively cheap pair of shoes as a 'son of a whore', demanding that he come back with a pair worth at least 13 times as much.

An unfortunate accident? William's death while hunting in the 'New Forest'

William Rufus portrayed in the 13th-century *Historia Anglorum*

Unhappy end William Rufus was shot while hunting in the 'New Forest' his father had created. Hunting accidents were common. William's brother Richard had also been killed hunting there. Supposedly Walter Tirel, one of William's knights, missed his shot at a deer, hitting the King instead. Tirel maintained his innocence. William's brother Henry was in the hunting party, and moved swiftly to claim the treasury and the throne.

Maybe a myth? Worried that the King had died a sinner, one of his huntsmen gave William the last rites by pushing flowers into his mouth.

What kind of ruler?

William Rufus (the Red) was his father's favourite, and although bequeathed England by the Conqueror, he had none the less to make sure he arrived ahead of his elder brothers to seize power when his father died. A good soldier, William was admired by his men. He was less popular with the Church for his rejection of religion and misappropriation of church revenues. His debaucheries were described 'as hateful to God and men' and the chronicler William of Malmesbury described the court where it was customary for young men 'to mince their gait and walk with loose gestures and half naked'.

Henry I 1100-35

Opportunist youngest son of William the Conqueror

Henry I, a scholarly king who proved to be a wise ruler

What kind of ruler?

After seizing power while his eldest brother's body was still warm, the studious Henry proved overall to be a wise ruler and a skilled diplomat. He reformed the administration and was nicknamed 'beauclerc' (good scholar) as he read Latin and studied English Law. However, he did have a wild side, fathering at least 21 illegitimate children.

Useful factfile

Born Late 1068, Selby in Yorkshire

Died 1 December 1135, aged 67, St Denis-le-Fermont, near Rouen, France. Buried at Reading Abbey

Crowned 6 August 1100, Westminster Abbey

Parents William the Conqueror and Matilda of Flanders

Married 1 Edith, who was renamed Matilda in honour of Henry's mother, 1100 (died 1118); 2 Adeliza, 1122

Children A son William and daughter Matilda (by Edith) were his only legitimate children. William was drowned in 1120, and Henry designated Matilda his heir, while leaving his illegitimate sons to fight amongst themselves

Royal scandal Henry was a witness to his elder brother William II's 'accidental' death from a stray arrow while out hunting. Recognising his chance, Henry galloped to Winchester to lay claim to the treasury, ensuring he would be crowned the next king before his older brother, Robert, could return from crusade.

Greatest tragedy In 1120 the King and his court were returning victorious from a battle in France. A new vessel *The White Ship* was offered to the King and he suggested his only son, William, aged 17 and his companions, travel in it. The young men were in high spirits, and the ship's captain and crew allegedly joined in the celebratory drinking, with disastrous results. The ship sailed late, and in the darkness hit a rock. Of the three hundred men on board, all but one, a butcher's son, was drowned. It is said that after this, Henry never smiled again.

Unhappy end In 1135 Henry, fit and well for his age, was staying at a hunting lodge in Normandy. In a good mood, he ordered a huge plate of his favourite food, lamprey eels, against his doctor's advice. He fell sick and died almost immediately from a bad bout of food poisoning, so shocking those around him that they attributed his death to a 'surfeit of lampreys'.

'this repast bringing on ill-humours, and violently exciting similar symptoms'

Henry of Huntingdon on the King's last meal

A coin struck during the reign of Henry III bearing his likeness

Stephen

1135-7 (deposed) restored 1141-54

Useful factfile

Born c1097

Crowned First on 22 December 1135, Westminster Abbey and again 25 December 1141 at Canterbury Cathedral

Died 25 October 1154, aged 57, at Dover. Buried Faversham Abbey

Parents Stephen, Count of Blois and Chartres and Adela, one of William the Conqueror's daughters

Married Matilda of Boulogne, 1125

Children Three sons including Eustace, his heir; two daughters and at least five illegitimate children

Handsome and chivalrous, Stephen was probably just too nice to be king

Biggest challenge His cousin Matilda. She wanted the throne, and fought Stephen fiercely. Despite being captured twice she escaped, once famously dressing in a white cloak and slipping away from a besieged Oxford during a snowstorm. In 1141 she captured Stephen and was declared 'Lady of the English' but before she could be crowned Stephen's followers captured her brother. He was exchanged for Stephen and the barons ceased to support her.

Toughest decision To surrender gracefully. Matilda's son, Henry, continued her quest for the crown. However, after Stephen's wife died, followed by his son and heir, Eustace, the fight went out of the King. In what must have been a relief to all concerned, he announced that Henry would be his heir.

'He was adept at the martial arts but in other respects little more than a simpleton'

Walter Map

Stephen's feisty cousin Matilda who challenged his claim to the throne

King Stephen enjoying the medieval pastime of hawking

What kind of ruler?

Stephen's reign was one of turmoil, even anarchy during the years between 1139 and 1145. He claimed power after Henry I died, saying that on his deathbed, his uncle had named him heir in preference to Henry's daughter Matilda. Stephen's feisty cousin, backed by her husband, Godfrey of Anjou, immediately challenged his claim. For the next 20 years Stephen and Matilda engaged in a vicious civil war for the crown, with neither side able to strike the decisive blow.

Palace connections

The Constable of the **Tower of London** during Stephen's reign was Geoffrey de Mandeville, who played a dangerous game, switching allegiances between Matilda and Stephen throughout the civil war. Through it all Stephen managed to keep control of the Tower but Geoffrey escaped to East Anglia where he was eventually killed during a skirmish.

Henry II
1154-89

The royal seal
of Henry II

Henry II debating with Archbishop Thomas Becket,
later murdered in Canterbury Cathedral

Henry in a detail
taken from a
14th-century
manuscript

What kind of ruler?

Henry's finest hour was finally establishing his claim to
his parents' lands. By inheritance, conquest and marriage
he pulled together an empire which included England,
overlordship of Wales, Ireland, Scotland and Brittany, plus
Normandy, Anjou, Maine and Aquitaine – considerably
more of France than was held by the French king.

Empire builder, law-giver and lover; too often betrayed by his volcanic temper and dysfunctional family

Useful factfile

Born 5 March 1133, Le Mans, County of Maine, France

Crowned 19 December 1154, Westminster Abbey

Died 6 July 1189, aged 56, at Chinon, France. Buried Fountevrault Abbey, France

Parents Geoffrey Plantagenet, Count of Anjou and the Empress Matilda, daughter of Henry I of England

Married Eleanor of Aquitaine, 1152

Children four sons: Henry (the Young King); Richard (the Lionheart, King of England); Geoffrey (Count of Brittany), John (Lackland, King of England); three daughters, Matilda, Eleanor, Joanna, and several illegitimate children including William Longespee, Earl of Salisbury

'Will no one rid me of this turbulent priest?'

Allegedly said by Henry II about his friend Archbishop Thomas Becket. It was interpreted literally by a group of Henry's knights who, eager to gain favour, rushed to Canterbury to murder Becket in the cathedral on 29 December 1170

Likes Action. He moved so fast his courtiers joked he must be able to fly. He preferred to stand rather than sit down. An eye-witness wrote, 'He always has a bow, sword, spear or arrow in his hands, unless he is in his council or reading.'

Dislikes At various points, most of his family. He faced civil wars with all his sons, and his wife, Eleanor. Young Henry died in the middle of one civil war, Eleanor was imprisoned, Geoffrey was accidentally killed in a tournament while plotting with the King of France in Paris. Henry died heartbroken when he discovered his favourite son, John, had joined in the rebellion.

Weird claim to fame Experimented with having his eldest son crowned king in his own lifetime. For a while England thus had two King Henrys, distinguished by contemporaries as 'the old King' and 'the young King'. Perhaps predictably, the only result was war between the alternative monarchs, ending (briefly) when young Henry died, then his siblings continued the fight without him.

Vices Extremely bad-tempered. Apoplectic with rage, he would throw himself on the floor, tear his bedding to pieces and chew the straw stuffing.

Should be ashamed of Becket's murder. Henry was, in fact, overcome with remorse for inadvertently bringing about the death of his friend. He walked barefoot to Canterbury where he allowed the monks to scourge him at the tomb of the archbishop, now a saint.

Royal scandal As if marrying Eleanor of Aquitaine two months after his rival the King of France divorced her wasn't scandal enough, Henry went on to have several mistresses. Most famous was 'Fair' Rosamund Clifford, for whom he built an exotic pleasure palace at Woodstock. Court gossips linked him romantically with his son's fiancée, whom he kept at court but refused to allow to marry.

Legacy His legal reforms and well-managed judicial system still form the basis of English Common Law.

The Plantagenets
Richard I 1189-99

The royal seal of Richard the Lionheart

A fabulous military adventurer, tough, glamorous and a brilliant general

Useful factfile

Born 8 September 1157, Beaumont Palace, Oxford

Crowned 3 September 1189, Westminster Abbey; celebrations horrifically marred by the massacre of London Jews forbidden to attend the ceremony, and subsequent massacres in Lincoln, Norwich and York

Died 6 April 1199, aged 42, in Aquitaine, France. Buried Fontevrault Abbey, Anjou

Parents Henry II and Eleanor of Aquitaine. Richard, their third son, was his mother's favourite, but he had a less happy relationship with his brothers and father

Married Berengaria of Navarre, daughter of Sancho VI, King of Navarre, in Cyprus, 1191. Richard's queen never set foot in England. It is claimed, although disputed, that Richard was homosexual and this was a marriage urged upon him by his mother

Children None

Finest hour At the age of 22 Richard won his first decisive military battle by capturing Talliebourg – a fortress that many said was impregnable. Richard used speed of troop movement and surprise attack as his highly successful battle tactic.

Marriage On her way by sea to meet him, Richard's bride-to-be Berengaria's ship was blown off course in a storm, and ended up in Cyprus, where it was plundered. Richard took swift revenge, conquering the island in under a month and marrying Berengaria there. He soon sold the island to the Templars to help fund his crusade.

Maybe a myth? In 1192 Richard was captured by Duke Leopold of Austria, and imprisoned in a secret location. Richard's friend and squire, a troubadour known as Blondel the Minstrel, set out to search Europe for his master. One day, while pausing outside a castle, Blondel began to sing one of Richard's favourite songs, and was amazed to hear a familiar voice joining in from a castle window high above. Blondel had found the King! Richard was released in 1194 and returned home to his faithful Blondel.

Unhappy end Rather carelessly, Richard allowed himself to come within range of an archer while laying siege to the castle of Chalus-Chabrol in France. He was hit in the shoulder and, despite the King claiming the wound was superficial, gangrene set in and he died within days. Richard's 'lion' heart was buried at Rouen and his body taken to the family vault at Fontevrault.

'Few English kings have played so small a part in the affairs of England and so large a part in the affairs of Europe as Richard I'

Professor Christopher Brooke

A statue of the crusader King outside the Houses of Parliament

What kind of ruler?

Leaving aside his crusading skills, as King of England Richard was a disaster. Despite spending only a few months of his ten-year rule in England (the least of any English monarch) Richard has become one of our most famous kings – known as 'Lionheart' largely because of his valour on the battlefield. Spending most of his time on the Third Crusade, Richard left his brother, John, as Regent. John eventually succeeded him.

Palace connections

While Richard was on crusade, William Longchamp, the Bishop of Ely and Richard's Chancellor, took care of the **Tower of London**. He set to work and doubled the size of the fortress and installed new defences. However, when John laid siege to the Tower hoping to gain control of his brother's crown, Longchamp was forced to surrender due to a lack of supplies!

John
1199-1216

The king who agreed to Magna Carta

Useful factfile

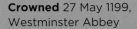

Born 24 December 1167 in Beaumont, Oxford

Crowned 27 May 1199, Westminster Abbey

Died 18 October 1216, aged 48, at Newark Castle. Buried Worcester Cathedral

Parents Henry II and Eleanor of Aquitaine

Married 1 Isabel of Gloucester, 1189 (divorced 1199); 2 Isabella of Angoulême, 1200

Children Two sons, including Henry (later Henry III) and three daughters

Palace connections

The **Tower of London** was attacked by John's forces in 1191, during the reign of his absentee brother, Richard. The defences were already being strengthened and they held firm. The Bell Tower may have been built in John's reign. He was a frequent resident of the Tower, and the first recorded reference to a lion-keeper dates from his reign.

Also known as John had two nicknames, Lackland, because his father had given him no landed inheritance, and Softsword, earned after the French invaded Normandy and Anjou in 1203 following John's murder of his nephew Arthur of Brittany.

Greatest loss King John is always said to have lost the Crown Jewels in the Wash – a source of schoolboy humour for generations. Taking his final journey from Norfolk to Lincolnshire and Nottinghamshire in October 1216, John sent his baggage train by a different route and it was lost in the quicksand when crossing the river.

Defining moment Magna Carta. John's reign had witnessed such aggressive exploitation of both the weak and the powerful that by 1212 he had precipitated a crisis of war and strife that lasted until his death four years later. War with France was followed by a baronial rebellion in England; having lost London to the rebels, John was forced to negotiate and seal Magna Carta (the Great Charter) at Runnymede on the Thames, 10-15 June 1215.

Legacy Magna Carta. A long and critical commentary on John's inept government, Magna Carta came to be regarded as a fundamental statement of English liberties. The English barons, who had no adult male Plantagenet to promote as their leader, radically devised a wide-ranging programme of reform for 'all free men of the realm and their heirs for ever'. Magna Carta passed into political myth, and was invoked in the lead-up to civil war in the 17th century and in the suffrage reform movement of the 19th century.

Unhappy end After allegedly losing the Crown Jewels and all his treasures in the Wash on his way to Lincoln, John caught a fever, not helped by his gluttonous consumption of peaches and new cider. He succumbed to dysentery, dying a few days later.

Screen appearances The most memorable was Claude Rains as the villainous John in *The Adventures of Robin Hood*, 1938.

'By God's feet'

John, much given to 'ribald and blasphemous remarks', was particularly fond of this oath, claimed chronicler Matthew Paris

What kind of ruler?

Deeply flawed, John was described as 'nature's enemy' by William of Newburgh, a contemporary historian with a soft spot for zombie stories! John was a desperately weak and poor king, who was always trying to shine in the shadow of his father, Henry II, and his brother, Richard 'the Lionheart'. His reign ended with the savage critique of his government in Magna Carta – and in civil war.

The King pictured with his dogs in a medieval hunting scene

The Plantagenets
Henry III
1216-72

The elephant presented to Henry III by King Louis IX of France in 1255. It was kept at the Tower of London

The elephant presented to Henry III by King Louis IX of France in 1255. It was kept at the Tower of London

Useful factfile

Born 1 October 1207, Winchester

Crowned 28 October 1216, Gloucester Abbey and again at Westminster, 17 May 1220

Died 16 November 1272, aged 65, at Westminster. Buried Westminster Abbey

Parents King John and Queen Isabella of Angoulême

Married Eleanor of Provence, 1236

Children Six sons, including Edward (later Edward I) and three daughters

Palace connections

Henry expanded the **Tower of London** beyond the Roman city walls, and built magnificent royal lodgings and a mighty curtain wall defended by mural towers. In 1240 he had the Tower's great keep painted white, making it the 'White Tower'. Henry kept an elephant (the first seen in England) and a white bear, diplomatic gifts from the kings of France and Norway, at the Tower of London.

Crowned aged nine, Henry grew up with a somewhat exalted (and unjustified) sense of his royal abilities

Weird claim to fame Henry idolised Saint-King Edward the Confessor, who it was thought had miraculously expelled worms from tumours in a woman's neck, and followed his hero's example. Henry became the first king to establish 'touching for the king's evil' as a royal tradition, and enthusiastically claimed the ability to cure victims of scrofula simply by touching or making the sign of the cross over them.

Greatest extravagance Henry loved extravagant decoration and accounts survive of his expenditure on elaborate thrones, brightly-coloured works of art and a great bed at Westminster Palace. This had paintings of the coronation of Edward the Confessor and two armed guards at its head, and was held up by green painted columns, spangled with gilt stars.

Should be ashamed of An unbecoming show of greed as a new father (he didn't have a general reputation for greed, more as a spendthrift); an anecdote from the birth of his son Edward at Westminster describes the King checking all birthday gifts received from the nobility of London. Those presents deemed not expensive enough were returned with contempt. The King's anger was only appeased when each person had given a satisfactory gift! According to chronicler Matthew Paris, a witty courtier is said to have remarked 'God gave us this child, but the king sells him to us'.

A highly flattering effigy of the King in Westminster Abbey

Henry at his first coronation in 1216

What kind of ruler?

Pious, charitable Henry identified with St Edward the Confessor and rebuilt Westminster Abbey to house his shrine and a royal mausoleum. Henry is often perceived as a weak and vacillating ruler for his lack of military might, but he was careful to be seen as a champion of the poor, sometimes feeding up to five hundred paupers a day. He favoured his Provencal wife's family and the company of his half-brothers to the chagrin of the English baronage, and was embroiled in a civil war until his son defeated Simon de Montfort at the Battle of Evesham in 1265. An enthusiastic builder of castles, domesticated Henry had a penchant for comfortable, brightly-painted rooms, liberally sprinkled with gilded stars.

Edward I
1272-1307

Edward I and his beloved first wife, Eleanor of Castile

Tall, warlike, yet heartbroken by the death of his wife

Nicknames Also known as 'Longshanks', for his great height 1.88m (6' 2") and 'the Hammer of the Scots' for his relentless campaigning north of the border.

Big battles Edward's armies defeated the Scots in 1296 – King John Balliol was imprisoned at the Tower. Edward notoriously stole the Scottish Stone of Destiny, and had it housed within a new coronation throne at Westminster Abbey, where it remained until 1996. William Wallace fought back and crushed the King's armies at the battle of Stirling Bridge in 1297. Edward defeated Prince Llywelyn of Wales in 1276 and 1282, and swiftly consolidated his victory by building a series of impregnable castles in north Wales.

Loves Edward adored his first wife Eleanor of Castile, who had accompanied him on crusade. When she died in 1209 (from a fever contracted during her journey to the north of England to visit him) Edward was heartbroken. He said of her 'whom living we dearly cherished, and whom dead we cannot cease to love'. To commemorate her he erected the 'Eleanor Crosses' – 12 monuments with sculptures of the Queen – at all the places where her funeral cortège rested. A 19th-century copy of one can be seen at Charing Cross in London and some original ones still survive across the country.

Should be ashamed of In 1290, Edward expelled the Jews from England, causing them great hardship and sorrow. Many had previously been imprisoned at the Tower, on charges of illegally clipping edges off silver coins – how many were actually guilty is unknown.

Useful factfile

Born 17/18 June 1239 at the Palace of Westminster

Crowned 19 August 1272, Westminster Abbey

Died 13 July 1307, aged 68, at Burgh by Sands, near Carlisle. Buried Westminster Abbey

Parents Henry III and Queen Eleanor of Provence

Married 1 Eleanor of Castile, 1254 (died 1290); 2 Margaret of France, 1299

Children Six surviving, including Edward, (later Edward II) of 14 children by Eleanor of Castile; three by Margaret of France

What kind of ruler?

Edward was a warrior king, who successfully conquered Wales, and fought the French, but who also established an enduring legal system in England. He had crusaded in the Holy Land in his youth, and defeated his father's enemies when still a prince. Happily married to Eleanor of Castile since a teenager and distraught at her death, Edward then wed a French princess, nearly 40 years his junior. Ever the fighting man, Edward died at Burgh by Sands, en route to make yet more war with the Scots.

Palace connections

Edward I was a great castle builder. He subdued north Wales with his massive and sophisticated fortifications at Caernarvon and elsewhere, and turned the **Tower of London** into a 'concentric' castle. He ringed it with a huge curtain wall and a moat, and built an impregnable land entrance to the fortress, as well as adding a palatial set of royal lodgings facing out across the River Thames. Edward established a branch of the Royal Mint at the Tower, and the nation's coinage was manufactured there for over five hundred years.

One of the 12 'Eleanor Crosses' commemorating Edward's first queen

Edward II 1307-27

Described at the time as 'fair of body and great of strength', Edward proved to be of little intellect or guile

Useful factfile

Born 25 April 1284 at Caenarvon Castle, Wales

Crowned 25 February 1308, Westminster Abbey

Died Murdered 21 September 1327, aged 43, at Berkeley Castle, Gloucester. Buried Gloucester Cathedral

Parents Edward I and Eleanor of Castile. Edward was their youngest (and only surviving male) child. He was the first heir to the throne to be given the title Prince of Wales, in 1301

Married Isabella of France, 1308

Children Two sons including Edward (later Edward III) and two daughters, and possibly one illegitimate child

What kind of ruler?

Edward's sexual indiscretions brought about his eventual downfall, his renunciation of the throne and his gruesome murder. His tragic, war-wracked reign was a disastrous turning point in medieval politics.

Dangerous liaisons In the early years of Edward's reign the barons proved fractious, angered by his homosexual infatuation with his favourite, Piers Gaveston. Edward accepted the barons' demands of 1311 that he institute reform and Gaveston was exiled; Gaveston returned in 1312, civil war broke out, and he was murdered. After 1320 Hugh Despenser became the royal favourite and a hated figure. Edward was forced to abdicate in 1327, after which Despenser and his family were executed.

Big battles Robert Bruce and his Scottish army defeated the English forces at Bannockburn on 24 June 1314. The only occasion that the Scots defeated the English when they were led by their king, Bannockburn is still famous within Scottish nationalism. At the Battle of Boroughbridge in 1322 Edward secured one of his rare victories. Defeating his cousin, Thomas of Lancaster, who had effectively ruled the country since Bannockburn, Edward then indulged in an orgy of judicial killing of his opponents (and Gaveston's murderers).

Biggest mistake Distressing his wife. Queen Isabella, sent to France in 1324 to discuss peace with her brother Charles IV, was so disgusted with her husband that she refused to return. She only came back two years later, with her lover Roger Mortimer and at the head of an invasion force. Edward's fate was sealed.

Unhappy end In January 1327 Edward II abdicated in favour of his teenage son. But he still represented a threat while alive. After being imprisoned at Berkeley Castle he was almost certainly murdered – and the story persists that the murder instrument was a red hot poker inserted in his rectum.

Edward's tomb effigy, complete with graffiti

Palace connections

The **Tower of London** was largely neglected during Edward II's reign, although he did use it as a place of refuge during the civil wars that raged. This was, however, the period when the Tower's role as a place for safeguarding state and legal records was established, with the Chapel in the White Tower fitted out for document storage.

A detail from an early 14th-century manuscript showing Edward with crown and sceptre

It is said that the 'she-wolf' Queen Isabella had Edward's heart removed from his body and put in a silver case. Her ferocious reputation was later epitomised in Thomas Gray's *The Bard* (1757)

'She-wolf of France, with unrelenting fangs, that tear'st the bowels of thy mangled mate'

'She-wolf' Isabella looking deceptively demure

31

The Plantagenets
Edward III 1327-77

A great and popular king, much romanticised by later chroniclers

A romantic image of Edward, from the east window of York Minster, 1405-8 (detail)

Edward and his wife, Philippa of Hainault

What kind of ruler?

As a teenager, Edward overthrew the domination of his mother, Isabella, and her lover, Roger Mortimer, to become one of the most successful military monarchs in English history. Edward was fascinated by chivalry and loved fighting in tournaments as well as on the battlefield. He was happily married to Philippa of Hainault, although his later years were dominated by his mistress Alice Perrers.

Edward III with his eldest son Edward, the 'Black Prince'

Lucky escape Edward and his court had to leave London to escape the Black Death in 1348-9, although his teenage daughter died from it in Bordeaux (an English territory at the time), as did his infant son, Thomas, but the rest of the royal family remained unscathed. The virulent bubonic plague swept through Europe, and almost a third of the population of England died.

Big battles Edward's reign saw the beginning of what became known as the 'Hundred Years War'. He spectacularly defeated Philippe VI at Crécy in northern France in 1346. His son, the Black Prince took the next French king, Jean II, prisoner at the Battle of Poitiers in 1356.

Legacy Edward founded the Order of the Garter – a chivalric military order of 26 knights, dedicated to the Virgin Mary and St George and modelled on the Arthurian Knights of the Round Table. Religious services were provided in the new Chapel of St George at Windsor Castle, which the King had rebuilt in magnificent style. The Order still exists, and many former Prime Ministers are Garter Knights. The 'garter' is thought to mean a sword belt.

The Plantagenets

Richard II 1377-99
(abdicated)

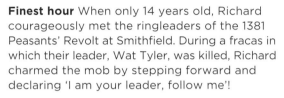

The first monarch to insist on being called 'Royal Majesty' (previously just 'your Grace')

Useful factfile

Born 6 January 1367 in Bordeaux

Crowned 16 July 1377, Westminster Abbey. Forced to abdicate 29 September 1399

Died Around 14 February 1400, aged 33, Pontefract Castle, Yorkshire. Buried initially at Kings Langley, then remains moved to Westminster Abbey

Parents Edward, the Black Prince (eldest son of Edward III), and Joan 'The Fair Maid of Kent'

Married 1 Anne of Bohemia, 1382 (died 1394); 2 Isabella of France (a 7-year-old, who outlived her husband), 1396

Children None

Finest hour When only 14 years old, Richard courageously met the ringleaders of the 1381 Peasants' Revolt at Smithfield. During a fracas in which their leader, Wat Tyler, was killed, Richard charmed the mob by stepping forward and declaring 'I am your leader, follow me'!

Greatest extravagance Richard was so distraught at the death of his first wife, Anne of Bohemia, that he had Sheen Palace, where she died, burnt to the ground.

Prominent courtiers Geoffrey Chaucer, author of *The Canterbury Tales*, was Richard's Clerk of the King's Works and supervised the building of the wharf at the Tower of London.

Aesthetic legacy Richard commissioned the magnificent wooden-vaulted roof of Westminster Hall and the exquisite painting of The Wilton Diptych, now at the National Gallery.

Unhappy end Richard was taken from the Tower just before Christmas 1399 to Pontefract Castle. Chroniclers agree when he died, but disagree about how it happened. Some say that he was deliberately starved to death; others that he starved himself. Others declared that Richard was hacked to pieces, and it is this version that Shakespeare dramatised.

Scenes from the Peasants' Revolt: the young King witnesses the death of Wat Tyler (left) and then faces down the rebels (right)

What kind of ruler?

Richard II came to the throne as a child, and presided over a reign of see-sawing power between himself and a rebellious nobility. Initially popular and displaying great courage during the Peasants' Revolt, Richard later helplessly watched many of his closest friends and advisors executed. Afterwards, Richard took revenge on those who had challenged his God-given right to rule. The King's high-handed behaviour earned him bitter enemies, and he was usurped by Henry Bolingbroke in 1399. Richard's downfall and suspicious death were immortalised in *Richard II* – Shakespeare's play, written two centuries later.

Palace connections

The **Tower of London** looms large in Richard II's life. He began and ended his reign there. At 10 years old, and clothed all in white, he embarked upon his glittering coronation procession from the Tower. Captured in 1399, Richard returned to the castle as a prisoner and was forced to abdicate. A chronicle recorded that the King laid his crown upon the ground and resigned his throne to God rather than the usurper, Henry Bolingbroke.

The Plantagenets

Henry IV 1399-1413

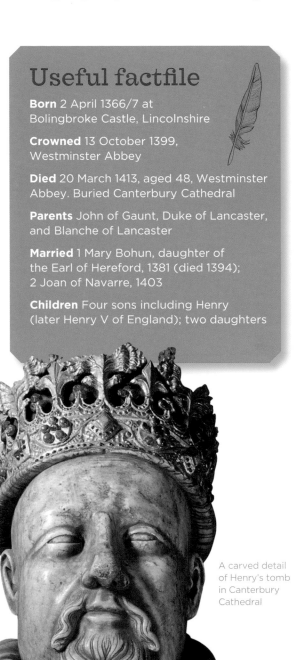

A carved detail of Henry's tomb in Canterbury Cathedral

Useful factfile

Born 2 April 1366/7 at Bolingbroke Castle, Lincolnshire

Crowned 13 October 1399, Westminster Abbey

Died 20 March 1413, aged 48, Westminster Abbey. Buried Canterbury Cathedral

Parents John of Gaunt, Duke of Lancaster, and Blanche of Lancaster

Married 1 Mary Bohun, daughter of the Earl of Hereford, 1381 (died 1394); 2 Joan of Navarre, 1403

Children Four sons including Henry (later Henry V of England); two daughters

Claim to fame Chivalrous crusader and pilgrim, a model for Chaucer's Knight in *The Canterbury Tales*.

Should be ashamed of Henry made burning heretics part of English law.

Finest hour His victory in 1403 at the Battle of Shrewsbury, over Henry Hotspur, son of the Earl of Northumberland. It is alleged Henry used body-doubles in battle, disguised with his own coat of arms, to act as targets for enemy attacks.

Celebrity victim His cousin, Richard II. He imprisoned Richard in the Tower of London, forced him to resign the crown, then declared himself king. Five months after Henry's coronation, Richard conveniently died in prison in Pontefract Castle.

Virtues Top jouster of his time.

Vices A bad record of broken promises not to invade, not to take the throne, not to kill Richard II, not to kill Richard's supporters without trial, not to behead the Archbishop of York, not to levy taxes...

Literary achievement Henry popularised the official use of English instead of French. He made his claim to the throne in Parliament in English and brought his sons up as English speakers. He was the first king to own an English translation of the Bible.

Artistic legacy Henry adopted a coat of arms quartering three gold English lions with three gold French fleurs-de-lis. This strikingly simple and elegant design was used by all kings and queens of England for the next 200 years, making it the most enduring version of the royal arms.

Nasty diseases Henry seems to have had few qualms about getting rid of Richard II, but after executing the Archbishop of York (whom he had promised to spare), his health went into sharp decline. According to contemporaries, God had punished him with leprosy. He had been king for barely seven years before his condition degenerated so much he had to virtually retire from government. In his will, written in English, he described himself as 'a sinful wretch' whose 'life I have mispended'.

Unhappy end Wracked by remorse, but unable to make a promised second pilgrimage to Jerusalem to die, the ailing king was carried to the Jerusalem Chamber in Westminster Abbey for his final hours.

Chivalrous adventurer who became a treacherous usurper, riddled with guilt and disease

Henry IV, the crusader king, in a late 16th-century oil painting by an unknown artist

What kind of ruler?

Henry Bolingbroke, as he was known, was banished into exile by a suspicious Richard II. Furious, Henry invaded and Richard succumbed within six weeks. Having convinced Parliament of his eligibility to the throne, Henry was crowned, but his reign proved increasingly stressful as he struggled to keep his throne and control Parliament. His health swiftly deteriorated; nevertheless he established a united kingdom for his son, Henry V.

The Plantagenets
Henry V 1413-22

Handsome Henry: actor Laurence Olivier in the 1944 film *Henry V*

Palace connections

Henry is believed to have worn the 'Black Prince's Ruby' (now in the Imperial State Crown, at the **Tower of London**) as part of the crown around his helmet at Agincourt. This was said to have been damaged when French knights tried to hack it away.

Physical oddity Henry is always illustrated by an image of him looking very gormless, with a pudding basin hair-cut. In fact this portrait dates from Tudor times. Contemporaries describe him as a tall, thin, long-faced and thick-haired young man, with a lithe physique which made him a superb runner.

Personal style When two quarrelling lords were brought before him while he was having his dinner, he declared that if they had not made up their differences before he had finished eating his oysters, they would both be hanged. Needless to say agreement was soon reached.

Royal scandal Impatient to get started, Henry took up the crown from beside his father's deathbed, to see how it fitted.

Finest hour The Battle of Agincourt, 25 October 1415. Heroic English bowmen destroyed the French knights. A much reduced English army, riddled with disease, faced the mighty French forces. Henry fought on foot alongside his soldiers.

Should be ashamed of Ordering the massacre of French prisoners during the battle of Agincourt.

Greatest victory In 1417, Henry landed in Normandy again. This time it was the King of England who conquered the Duchy of Normandy. He sealed his victory by marrying Catherine de Valois, the daughter of the King of France, whose heir he became. He captured Paris and finally made good the longstanding English claim to the French throne.

Wild youth who became England's heroic leader; lived fast, died young

Sense of humour Hearing that Henry was planning to invade, the King of France's son, the Dauphin, sent him a derisory gift of tennis balls, 'because he should have somewhat to play withal, for him and for his lords'. Henry replied by saying he would be sending back cannon-balls 'hard and great gun stones for the Dauphin to play withal'. Soon Henry and his army were at Harfleur, blasting great holes in the walls to make good the threat.

Unhappy end Henry caught dysentery while campaigning against the last pockets of French resistance. He was 36. He never got to see his son and heir, the future Henry VI, who was still in England, a baby, aged just 8 months.

A Tudor portrait of the King as a young man

What kind of ruler?

A resourceful and valiant solider, Henry was also a tireless administrator. His reign was one of the shortest of any English king since the Norman Conquest, but it was one of the most successful. Henry managed to hold together the English barons, at the same time regaining more lost territory than any other king.

The Plantagenets
Henry VI

1422-61 (deposed).
Restored 1470-1 (deposed again)

The wrong king at the wrong time

Useful factfile

Born 6 December 1421, at Windsor Castle

Crowned King of England, 5 November 1429, (aged 8) Westminster Abbey; King of France, 16 December 1431, Notre-Dame, Paris. (Henry VI was heir to the kingdom of France according to the Treaty of Troyes, but his French coronation was little more than a propaganda exercise – Charles VII had been crowned in Rheims over a year earlier)

Died 21 May 1471, aged 49, at the Tower of London. Buried first at Chertsey Abbey, later St George's Chapel, Windsor

Parents Henry V and Queen Catherine de Valois, daughter of Charles VI of France

Married Margaret of Anjou, 1445

Children Edward of Lancaster (d 1471)

Most charismatic rival The 17-year-old Joan of Arc, whose victory raising the siege of Orleans rallied French troops all over the country to regain the land captured by Henry's father.

Artistic achievements Henry was a great patron of architecture and learning, and founded Eton College and King's College, Cambridge whilst still in his twenties. Every year, representatives from these establishments attend the 'Lilies and Roses' ceremony on the evening of 21 May at the Tower of London, to commemorate his death, in the room where the unhappy king is said to have met his violent end.

What kind of ruler?

Henry VI was a pious, scholarly king who was precipitated into the tumultuous Wars of the Roses. Indecisive and prone to bouts of severe mental illness, poor melancholic Henry had to contend with the ambitions of his rival the Duke of York and his brood, the vacillations of the powerful Earl of Warwick (the Kingmaker), and the fierce determination of his queen to defend her husband and son's birthright.

Unhappy end Murder, or despair? Edward IV, the eventual victor of this stage of the Wars of the Roses, claimed that poor Henry had died of despair and ill health, brought about by his failures, the death of his son, and his wife's capture. However, it is recorded that Henry's body bled on the pavement of St Paul's Cathedral, where it lay 'open-visaged' so that people could be sure that he was really dead.

Coin depicting Henry's wife, Margaret of Anjou

Henry VI by an unknown
artist, c1540

Wars of the Roses 1455-85
These ferocious struggles for
power were fought for England
as the ultimate prize. Both
warring parties (the family of
Lancaster, whose symbol was
a red rose) and the family of
York (a white rose) claimed
Edward III as their royal ancestor,
so both wanted the crown of
England. Many bloody, but
undecisive battles were fought,
that culminated in the Battle
of Bosworth in 1485, in which
Richard III was killed and Henry
VII became king.

Palace connections

Henry began his reign, as his father and grandfather had before him, by
spending the night at the **Tower of London** on the eve of his coronation.
He created over 30 Knights of the Bath there, who escorted him with full
pomp to the ceremony. This vivid boyhood experience must have seemed
very distant when Henry returned to the Tower as a prisoner in 1465, where
he nevertheless lived in relative comfort for five years. Henry found himself briefly back on the
throne for six months, but was returned to his prison in spring 1471, after defeats at the battles
of Barnet and Tewkesbury, and the death of his son. Within a suspiciously short time, Henry
died, and later reports claim he had been murdered while at prayer in the Wakefield Tower.

The Plantagenets
Edward IV

1461-70 (deposed). Restored 1471-83

A late 16th-century portrait of Edward IV
by an unknown artist

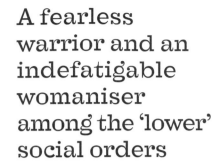

Big battles Edward was a fearless warrior from an early age, and triumphed over the forces of his Lancastrian rival, Henry VI, at the Battle of Towton in 1461. The powerful Earl of Warwick (called 'the Kingmaker') supported the new young king, but losing patience with him he changed sides and fought with the Lancastrian faction nine years later. The rebellious Earl was defeated at the Battle of Barnet on 14 April 1471, and on 4 May the forces of the imprisoned Henry VI's queen and son were demolished at the Battle of Tewkesbury.

Royal scandal Edward had an eye for a pretty face, and secretly married attractive widow, Elizabeth Woodville, his social inferior. Somewhat embarrassed by his impolitic behaviour, Edward kept the news from his advisors for several months. Once she was acknowledged as queen, Elizabeth's relatives were rewarded with court positions and advantageous marriages. Edward's marriage didn't put a stop to his philandering; he had many mistresses including Jane Shore, the divorced wife of a London merchant.

Artistic achievements Edward rebuilt the magnificent St George's Chapel at Windsor Castle, and was eventually buried there in 1483.

Useful factfile

Born 28 April 1442 at Rouen, Normandy

Crowned 28 June 1461, Westminster Abbey

Died 9 April 1483, aged 41, at Palace of Westminster. Buried St George's Chapel, Windsor

Parents Richard, Duke of York, and Duchess Cecily (Neville)

Married In secret, Elizabeth Grey, née Woodville, a widow with two sons, 1464

Children Seven daughters, including his eldest, Elizabeth who married Henry VII, and three sons. The eldest two 'disappeared' while at the Tower of London, shortly after the King's death. Two acknowledged illegitimate children and rumoured to have fathered many more

Alongside Edward and Elizabeth Woodville, stand the future kings, Richard III (in blue) and young Edward V (in red and ermine)

What kind of ruler?

A bold soldier, Edward IV was tall, handsome and affable. Decisive in battle, yet indolent in peacetime, this king made a politically unwise secret marriage, had many affairs, executed his brother and ultimately triumphed as the leader of the Yorkist faction in the Wars of the Roses. He over-indulged his taste for pleasure, and died at the age of 41, leaving his fragile young heir, also Edward, to inherit a crown ripe for the taking.

Palace connections

Edward had his brother, the Duke of Clarence, executed for treason at the **Tower of London** in 1478. Scandalous reports of the death suggested that he was drowned in a butt of malmsey wine. Edward's heir and also his second son Richard, disappeared mysteriously whilst at the Tower during their uncle's usurpation of the throne (see factfile). On a less dramatic note, Edward extended the castle by building an enormous brick bulwark to defend the western entrance to the Tower. The foundations of this structure still survive.

The Plantagenets
Edward V
1483
(never crowned)

Tragic youngster, enshrined in popular memory as one of the 'Princes in the Tower'

Edward and his brother Richard by the Victorian artist John Millais, 1878

As a young Prince of Wales, Edward was cosseted in his own household at Ludlow Castle. On the death of his father, Edward became king at the age of 12; in reality a pawn in the hands of his battling relatives, who sought to rule the country during his minority. Edward and his younger brother Richard, Duke of York soon became 'inconvenient', and disappeared without trace. It is probable that the boys were murdered on the orders of their uncle Richard, Duke of Gloucester. Today the boys are popularly known as the 'The Princes in the Tower'.

Royal scandal The King's uncle Richard, Duke of Gloucester, who had sent the boys to the Tower 'for their safety', had them declared illegitimate on 22 June 1483, and cleared the way for his usurpation of the throne – he was crowned Richard III on 6 July.

Legacy 19th-century artists were gripped by the tragic tale, and painters such as Paul Delaroche, John Millais and James Northcote depicted the 'Little Princes' at various stages during their imprisonment and murder at the Tower.

Unhappy ends While the cause of death is unknown, Thomas More wrote a heavily biased account of the boys' murder, and claimed that they had been smothered to death. This interpretation of events was used by Shakespeare in his play *Richard III*.

Useful factfile

Born 2 November 1470 at Westminster

Crowned Became king on the death of his father on 9 April 1483, but remained uncrowned – his coronation was postponed and then abandoned

Died Probably murdered at the Tower of London, September 1483, aged 12. Buried at the Tower; later reinterred at Westminster Abbey

Parents Edward IV and Elizabeth Woodville

The murder of the innocents? The terrible scene as imagined by painter James Northcote in the late 18th century

Palace connections

Edward V and his brother Richard were last seen playing in a garden at the **Tower of London**. What was then the 'Garden Tower' has since been interpreted as their prison and place of murder. The tragic events surrounding the disappearance and probable violent end of the brothers, is reflected in the change of the building's name, to the 'Bloody Tower' by the middle of the following century. Two skeletons, believed to be those of the murdered boys, were discovered under a demolished staircase in front of the White Tower in 1674, and were reburied on Charles II's orders in Westminster Abbey.

Richard III 1483-5

Laurence Olivier played the King as Shakespeare's theatrical villain in the 1955 film of the play *Richard III*

'Crookback' Richard was the last English monarch to die in battle

Physical oddity Shakespeare, using pro-Tudor sources, depicted Richard III as a dastardly villain, with a twisted body and a humped back. A portrait of Richard (painted after his death) was thought to record this deformity, but has subsequently been shown to have been altered to exaggerate his alleged imperfections.

Unhappy end Richard was killed in action at the Battle of Bosworth, charging bravely into the thick of the fighting but was quickly cut down. The victor, Henry Tudor, had his body buried without ceremony at a Leicester friary. During the Dissolution of the Monasteries in 1536, Richard's tomb was destroyed. In 2013, bones discovered under a car park in Leicester city were identified as belonging to the missing King, and reburied in Leicester Cathedral.

Useful factfile

Born 2 October 1452 at Fotheringhay Castle, Northamptonshire

Crowned 6 July 1483, Westminster Abbey

Died 22 August 1485, aged 33, at Bosworth Field fighting Henry Tudor. Buried originally at Greyfriars Abbey, Leicester, his remains now rest in Leicester Cathedral

Parents Richard, Duke of York, and Duchess Cecily (Neville)

Married Anne Neville, daughter of the Earl of Warwick and widowed daughter-in-law of Henry VI, 1472

Children Edward, Prince of Wales (d 1484), and two illegitimate children

What kind of ruler?

Brother to Edward IV, on the King's death Richard snatched his young nephew Edward V from his mother's family and, having had the boy king declared illegitimate, seized the throne for himself. Although often portrayed as an arch-villain, demonised by pro-Tudor Shakespeare and described as monstrously deformed by his opponents, Richard was a charismatic and successful military leader before he became king. He had an unpopular tendency to have his enemies executed without trial, and had to deny rumours of poisoning his wife.

A vivid portrait of Richard III, painted by an unknown artist c1480-1500. Shakespeare famously referred to him as 'Crookback' but there is little evidence to support this unflattering description

Palace connections

Many of the darker episodes in Richard's life took place at the **Tower of London**. His brother, the troublesome Duke of Clarence, had allegedly been executed there by being drowned in a butt of malmsey wine in 1478. Lord Hastings was executed without trial within the Tower's walls, for opposing Richard's plans to take the throne, and the usurped Edward V and his brother Richard rather conveniently disappeared, never to be seen again, while being held there.

The House of Tudor
Henry VII
1485-1509

A Welshman of action, turned shrewd financial planner

Best decision Once crowned, Henry made a smart move to strengthen his shaky position by marrying Elizabeth of York, thus uniting the houses of York and Lancaster. Elizabeth was the eldest daughter of Edward IV and after the mysterious disappearance of his two sons from the Tower of London she was the heir to Yorkist claims to the throne. Henry also fell passionately in love with her.

Plots Throughout Henry's reign he was plagued by 'pretenders' to the throne. The most persuasive of these was Perkin Warbeck, who claimed to be Richard, Duke of York, the younger of the two princes who disappeared at the Tower of London. Perkin's claim was supported by Charles VIII of France and Margaret of Burgundy (Edward IV's sister) who recognised him as her nephew and rightful heir to the throne. Despite landing in Cornwall and raising an army, Perkin was no match for Henry's forces, and a truce was signed. However, Henry's leniency backfired, and when Warbeck again tried to gather support he was held at the Tower of London, and eventually hanged at Tyburn in November 1499.

Legacy Henry VII was the first King of England to have a recognisable portrait of himself on a coin. In 1494 he appointed a highly-skilled German engraver to the Royal Mint, and in 1502 the first ever coin with a realistic portrait of the King went into circulation. For much of the population, this was the first time they had seen a picture of their monarch.

Henry VII (top left) with his wife Elizabeth of York (top right); son Henry VIII and Jane Seymour in the dynastic *Whitehall Mural* painted by Remigius van Leemput, 1669

Useful factfile

Born 28 January 1457 at Pembroke Castle

Crowned 30 October 1485, Westminster Abbey

Died 21 April 1509, aged 52, at Richmond Palace. Buried Westminster Abbey

Parents Edmund Tudor and Lady Margaret Beaufort

Married Elizabeth of York, 1486

Children Two sons: Arthur (d 1502) and Henry (later Henry VIII); two daughters Margaret and Mary and four other children who died in infancy

What kind of ruler?

Henry seized the crown by force from Richard III at the Battle of Bosworth. However, despite only a flimsy claim to the throne, Henry then held on to it for the next 24 years through a prompt, well-thought out marriage which united the houses of Lancaster and York, political skill and prudent (some said mean!) budgetary control. The arrival of the Tudors heralded a new age, and with Henry VII came increasing peace, prosperity and enlightenment. He rebuilt the Crown's finances and paved the way for a Tudor dynasty.

Palace connections

Henry VII used the **Tower of London** extensively. He held feasts and tournaments there to celebrate his victory over Richard III and also built more comfortable lodgings for himself and his family.

Henry VII by an unknown artist, c1550-1699

The House of Tudor

Henry VIII 1509-47

Hero or tyrant? The jury is still out after 500 years

Likes As a young man, Henry VIII placed more emphasis on sport and fun than on the duty of policy and ruling. Cardinal Wolsey, his Chief Minister, did that for him effectively. A cultured man, Henry was an accomplished musician and occasional composer. 'Pastime with good company' was his song and his motto.

Second son syndrome Henry's elder brother, Arthur, was due to inherit, but his premature death in 1502 catapulted Henry into the position of heir to the throne. Henry also took Arthur's young widow, Katherine of Aragon, as his wife, an act that would have huge consequences 21 years later.

Powerful men Henry's reign saw the rise from relatively humble origins of two great politicians and administrators: Thomas Wolsey, the churchman, later Cardinal, and Thomas Cromwell, created Earl of Essex. Each acquired a huge range of powers, and substantial wealth. Each fell spectacularly from grace in 1529 and 1540 respectively, victims of the political machinations around the King's marital history.

Near-death experience A bad fall when jousting in 1536 left the King unconscious for over two hours and made him abandon many sports. The accident may have altered his metabolism, and he grew monstrously fat.

Physical oddity The mature Henry had the most recognisable body profile of any monarch. A slim young man, by age 50 his massive chest measured 144cm (57in) and his waist a bloated 137cm (54in).

Useful factfile

Born 28 June 1491 at Greenwich Palace, London

Crowned 24 June 1509, Westminster Abbey

Died 28 January 1547, aged 55, at Whitehall Palace, London. Buried St George's Chapel, Windsor

Parents Henry VII and Elizabeth of York

Married 1 Katherine of Aragon, 1509 (annulled 1533); 2 Anne Boleyn, 1533 (executed 1536); 3 Jane Seymour, 1536 (died in childbirth 1537); 4 Anne of Cleves, 1540 (annulled 1540); 5 Catherine Howard, 1540 (executed 1542), 6 Kateryn Parr, 1543 (survived Henry)

Children Mary (later Mary I, by Katherine of Aragon); Elizabeth (later Elizabeth I, by Anne Boleyn); Edward (later Edward VI, by Jane Seymour) and many other children who died in infancy or were still born. One illegitimate child – possibly more.

What kind of ruler?

Many will argue that Henry VIII's was the single most important reign in English history. The break with Rome made England a Protestant nation, and the Dissolution of the Monasteries changed irreversibly the shape of land ownership and power. Parliament acquired greater authority than it had ever had before, and effective government was instituted throughout the country. Henry VIII helped make England into a European power. All this was played against the background of his six marriages, in a seemingly desperate race to gain a legitimate son and heir.

The monarch with the most recognisable body profile: Henry VIII after Hans Holbein

Palace connections

Hampton Court Palace was Henry's 'pleasure palace', which he turned into a fabulous centre of entertainment, feasting, jousting and hunting. Henry married his sixth wife, Kateryn Parr at Hampton Court. His son Edward was born at the palace in 1537; days later his mother Jane Seymour died there from birth complications. Henry imprisoned two of his wives, Anne Boleyn and Catherine Howard in the **Tower of London**. Both were executed on Tower Green.

Biggest extravagance The Field of Cloth of Gold in 1520 was an immensely lavish meeting with the French King Francis I. The 'Perpetual Peace' that was agreed when they met lasted a mere two years.

Celebrity victims Too many to list. Henry used accusations of treason and execution as instruments of terror and as convenient ways of disposing of discarded wives, favourites, politicians and rivals.

Palace connections:
Hampton Court Palace

Hampton Court is a mixed-up monument to the architectural tastes and ambitions of England's kings and queens. This hasn't always been valued as it is now

In 1833 a journalist suggested that: 'Except that Hampton Court was built by Wolsey, and occupied (as was Kensington) by William III, we know not of any classical or historical recollections that ought to redeem those two brick houses from the pickaxe'! Indeed, kings and queens themselves have always destroyed (or renovated) as much as they have built. In 1353, Edward III's royal retinue accidently set fire to the medieval manor house at Hampton Court, whilst in 1689 William III and Mary II planned the complete demolition of the Tudor palace!

Henry VIII's Hampton Court was – as it has remained ever since – a pleasure palace of elegant courtyards and royal apartments provided with parks (for hunting), gardens (for idling), a tiltyard (for jousting), tennis courts (for letting off steam) and bowling alleys (in lieu of weight-lifting at the gym). Henry was practising archery in the gardens when news reached him of the death of Cardinal Wolsey, his former chief minister, who had first begun the creation of this Tudor playground. Henry's newly royal palace grew and grew, often as he added or refurbished apartments for his successive wives. What self-respecting queen would want to live in her predecessor's rooms?

Elizabeth I didn't share her father's passion for architectural projects and the palace remained more-or-less unchanged until **Charles II**'s restoration in 1660. His new apartments (now lost) overlooked the parks and gardens, where, in preparation for his

honeymoon at the palace with his Portuguese queen, Catherine of Braganza, he commissioned a grand canal to be dug, lined with 'sweete rows of lime-trees' (today's Long Water).

On their arrival in England in 1688 **William III** and **Mary II** set about house (or palace) hunting. Taken with the setting of Hampton Court, they hoped to sweep away the old-fashioned buildings and raise an up-to-the-minute European palace, designed by Christopher Wren. However (and some might say fortunately), since William's wars with the French king, Louis XIV, had first call on the royal finances, only a third of Henry VIII's palace was finally

The magnificent vaulted ceiling of the Chapel Royal, installed in 1530

rebuilt (around today's elegant courtyard, Fountain Court). With William off campaigning on the Continent, Mary was left to supervise the work. Wren's son recalled how she 'pleased herself from time to time, in examining and surveying the drawings... and to give thereon her own judgement, which was exquisite'.

As Hampton Court fell out of royal use in the 18th century it attracted greater and greater numbers of tourists and visitors, many drawn to the Tudor parks and the baroque gardens. **Queen Victoria** formally opened the palace to the public in 1838. Only a few years later the palace was praised in the *Times* as, 'one of the very few English sights which can be thoroughly enjoyed by any humble individual at his own leisure and discretion. The admission is not only free of charge, but free of annoyance'.

Holbein's famous portrait of Henry VIII, 1536 (detail)

Edward VI 1547-53

Useful factfile

Born 12 October 1537 at Hampton Court Palace

Crowned 20 February 1547, aged 9, Westminster Abbey

Died 6 July 1553, aged 15, Greenwich Palace. Buried Westminster Abbey

Parents Henry VIII and Jane Seymour

Married never

Children none

What kind of ruler?

Edward succeeded to the throne aged 9, under the Protectorship of his uncle, Edward Seymour, Duke of Somerset. The young king, extensively educated and with strong opinions, was intellectually precocious and determined to make England Protestant. However, he was surrounded by ambitious, rival courtiers, chief among them John Dudley, Duke of Northumberland, who masterminded the brief, tragic reign of his daughter-in-law, Lady Jane Grey after the sickly Edward died, aged 15.

Pale-faced, small and skinny, devout Edward was 'God's imp'

Reforming zeal Archbishop Cramner and Edward's tutors were committed Protestants and they influenced the young King who became a reformer. He agreed to the creation of an English Book of Common Prayer, which was distributed in 1548, and commanded that Catholic images in stained glass, wood and stone be destroyed. Popular rebellions against the reforms were brutally repressed by the Duke of Somerset.

Royal scandal When it became clear that poor teenage Edward did not have long to live, the Duke of Northumberland was desperate to avoid Edward's Catholic sister Mary succeeding to the throne. Northumberland is said to have ordered Edward's doctors to administer enough arsenic to keep the boy alive long enough to sign papers creating the King's Protestant cousin – and Northumberland's daughter-in-law – Lady Jane Grey, the next monarch.

Edward's christening procession at Hampton Court Palace

Palace connections

Edward was born at **Hampton Court Palace**, where his father is said to have wept with joy when he first held him. Edward's magnificent christening ceremony was held in the newly redecorated Chapel Royal, and attended by over three hundred courtiers. The young Prince was carried in state from his rooms to the sound of trumpets. At his christening he was given the title of Duke of Cornwall.

Lady Jane Grey

Queen of England for nine days

Proclaimed Queen 10 July 1553 (never crowned), deposed on 19 July.

Died Executed for treason 12 February 1554, aged 16.

Buried The Tower of London.

Jane was married to the Duke of Northumberland's son, Guildford, and her father-in-law schemed to have her proclaimed the next Protestant heir on Edward VI's death instead of Henry VIII's daughter Mary. But there was much support for Mary, and in the fighting that followed Northumberland's forces were defeated; he was executed and Jane and Guildford were imprisoned in the Tower. Guildford, followed by poor innocent Jane, was executed for treason on 12 February 1554.

Like father, like son, the young Edward VI by Hans Holbein

The House of Tudor
Mary I
1553-8

A psychological mess, 'Bloody Mary' never recovered from her childhood

What kind of ruler?

Having been declared a bastard by her father and having had to endure banishment from court and separation from her beloved mother Katherine of Aragon, it was unlikely that Mary would make a kindly, tolerant monarch. The first Queen of England to be crowned and to rule in her own right. 'Bloody Mary' devoted a good deal of energy and cruelty to restoring what she called the true religion – Catholicism. However, burning over 300 Protestants at the stake did not make her any happier; her marriage to Philip of Spain did not lead to the conception of her longed-for child and, in the closing months of her reign, the English lost Calais – the last relic of a once proud empire.

Obsessions Mary, like her mother, was a committed Catholic. During her brother Edward VI's reign she resisted pressure to convert from Catholicism, nearly falling victim to a plot to make the Protestant Lady Jane Grey her brother's successor. Once Queen, she set about martyring Protestants, reversing reforms and reinstating some Catholic bishops, but she stopped short of restoring the land taken from the monasteries by her father.

Unpleasant affliction Small and short-sighted, poor Mary may have suffered a form of rhinitis that gave her foul-smelling breath, which didn't endear her to many.

Poor choice Mary chose the Catholic Philip of Spain as her husband, a political alliance that proved extremely unpopular and gave rise to a serious rebellion. Thomas Wyatt and his followers, unhappy at the marriage and the religious reform, marched on London in 1554 in an attempt to reinstate Lady Jane Grey as Protestant successor. The City of London held fast, and the rebels were defeated, while Mary was left with no choice but to have poor Jane Grey executed to stop further plotting.

Most difficult decision Agreeing, a few months before her death, that her half-sister Elizabeth should succeed her.

Unhappy end Soon after her marriage Mary and her doctors were convinced that she was pregnant, but they were wrong. Philip (who stayed away from his wife as much as possible) returned briefly in 1557 and Mary declared she was with child again despite being 41 by this stage. It appears that her swollen stomach may have contained a large tumour, and by the following year she had died.

'When I am dead, you will find Philip and Calais engraved upon my heart'

Mary and her somewhat reluctant husband Philip of Spain, thought to be painted by a follower of Antonio Mor, 1558

Palace connections

Mary was at **Hampton Court Palace** in 1554 when Spanish ambassors arrived to offer her the hand of King Philip II of Spain, which she accepted. A year later the court gathered at the palace to await the birth of Mary's baby. Mary's younger half sister Elizabeth was summoned, kept under close guard. However, the baby never came in what must have been a 'false pregnancy'

Elizabeth I
1558-1603

A gold medal of Elizabeth I by Nicholas Hilliard

The Virgin Queen who wanted 'everyone to be in love with her'

Nasty diseases In October 1562, Elizabeth succumbed to a severe bout of smallpox while staying at Hampton Court. It was thought she would die, but by the end of the month the indomitable Queen was out of bed and 'attending to the marks of her face to avoid disfigurement'.

Finest hour Her famously rousing speech to the troops at Tilbury on the approach of the Spanish Armada invasion fleet in 1588 began 'I know I have the body of a weak and feeble woman, but I have the heart and stomach of a king and of a king of England too.'

Celebrity victim Elizabeth reluctantly authorised the execution of her Catholic cousin, Mary, Queen of Scots on 8 February 1587. Elizabeth was to demonstrate great grief after the beheading and tried to blame her councillors.

Personal style A youthful beauty, the Queen fought the signs of ageing. She wore elaborate wigs to hide her thinning hair, covered her smallpox scars with white lead and is said to have rubbed urine into her face to combat wrinkles. It was even harder to hide her blackened teeth, rotted through her fondness for sugar. However, she had over three thousand magnificent frocks, many embroidered with gold thread and encrusted with jewels.

Useful factfile

Born 7 September 1533 at Greenwich Palace

Crowned 15 January 1559, Westminster Abbey

Died 24 March 1603, aged 69, at Richmond Palace. Buried Westminster Abbey

Parents Henry VIII and Anne Boleyn

Married Never

Children None

Palace connections

Elizabeth spent a frightening few months at the **Tower of London** in 1554 as a prisoner on suspicion of involvement in a Protestant rebellion against Catholic half-sister Mary I. She returned five years later to spend the night before her triumphant coronation procession to Westminster Abbey. The first banqueting house to be built at Whitehall Palace was constructed as a site for Elizabeth's doomed marriage negotiations with France. The marvels that Elizabeth had constructed for her pleasure at **Hampton Court Palace** included a fabulous room called 'Paradise', decorated with precious metals and gems to dazzle visitors. The Queen was also fond of a joke, and installed a new fountain at the palace that contained a secret device to squirt water at visitors standing nearby!

Elizabeth I, resplendent in coronation robes, painted by an unknown artist, c1559

What kind of ruler?

Elizabeth's start in life was not auspicious. Being born a girl, and not a son and heir for Henry VIII made her a great disappointment. She inherited her father's red hair, fiery temper and strong will, and probably could not remember her mother, who was executed when she was three. The ultimate survivor, Elizabeth outlived her Tudor half-siblings, and became queen, reigning for 44 years in what is often regarded as a 'golden age'. Despite several failed attempts to make a political marriage, Elizabeth eventually chose the single life, preferring to have favourites dancing attendance upon her, and trusted advisors to guide her Protestant kingdom through troubled times.

The House of Stuart
James I
1603-25

(King James VI of Scotland 1567-1625)

'The wisest fool in Christendom'

The young James with his mother Mary Queen of Scots

Useful factfile

Born 19 June 1566 at Edinburgh Castle

Crowned King of Scotland 29 July 1567 (aged 13 months) at Stirling Castle and King of England 25 July 1603 at Westminster Abbey

Died 27 March 1625, aged 58, at Theobalds Park, Hertfordshire. Buried Westminster Abbey

Parents Mary Queen of Scots and her second husband, Henry Stuart, Lord Darnley

Married Anna of Denmark

Children Five who survived infancy, including his eldest son Charles (later Charles I). and daughter Elizabeth, who married the Elector Palatine Frederick (from whom the Hanoverian kings of England were descended)

Royal scandal James's father, Darnley, was murdered soon after he was born. Darnley had previously collaborated in the murder of Mary's secretary and probable lover, David Rizzio; and Mary's third husband, Lord Bothwell, was implicated in Darnley's murder. A rising against the couple forced Mary to abdicate in favour of her infant son.

Favourites James's life and reign was filled with a succession of male favourites and lovers, notably Robert Carr, Earl of Somerset (from 1607), and George Villiers, Duke of Buckingham (from 1614). Each had a significant impact on court life and politics, as a focus of patronage and factional strife.

Obsessions James had very fixed and strident views on many subjects, and published them in a series of books and pamphlets. *Basilikon Doron* (1599) explained his vision of personal kingship. *Daemonologie* (1597) expressed his fascination with witchcraft and his patronage of the witch-craze. *A Counterblast to Tobacco* (1606) was one of the first anti-smoking pamphlets.

Legacy *The King James Bible* was published in 1611, the Authorised Version of the Bible in English, translated by bands of scholars. It was a hugely influential outcome of the 1604 Hampton Court Conference, called by the King to debate differences in religion.

Remember, remember The annual fifth November celebration of the discovery of the Gunpowder Plot and the execution of Guy Fawkes in 1605 is a tangible link to pro-Catholic religious terrorism. The foiled plot intended to blow up King, Parliament and Church at the State Opening of Parliament.

Physical oddities Known as a slobberer and semi-coherent speaker, James may have suffered from mild cerebral palsy. This is a more realistic diagnosis than the 'royal disease' porphyria, with which he has often been associated.

James I was a wilier and cannier monarch than the 'fool' tag suggests. He united the thrones of Scotland and England when he succeeded Elizabeth I in 1603, changing the direction of English history. He tried to keep the lid on many aspects of public life – religion, royal finances, and fractious parliamentary relations – that burst out again disastrously in Charles I's reign.

Palace connections

James I stayed at the **Tower of London** after he arrived in his new kingdom in 1603. He was the last monarch to stay at the fortress and particularly enjoyed watching the cruel animal displays there. As the instigator of Inigo Jones's dazzling classical **Banqueting House**, he has a particular place in the history of architectural patronage. **Hampton Court** was the setting for the religious conference of 1604, and the first performances by Shakespeare's acting company as the King's Men.

A coronation portrait of James I by Paul van Somer, c1620, with his new Banqueting House in the background

The magnificent Rubens' ceiling painting commissioned by Charles I, was installed in 1636

Palace connections:
The Banqueting House

The Banqueting House in present-day Whitehall, now surrounded by government offices and ministries, is the sole survivor of the legendary Palace of Whitehall, once the greatest palace of its time in Europe, but almost totally destroyed by fire in 1698

The first banqueting house on the site was a relatively flimsy, although magnificently decorated great hall, constructed for **Elizabeth I** in 1581. It was built to host the steady stream of ambassadors visiting the highly eligible young sovereign to negotiate marriage contracts. The timber framed hall was covered with canvas painted in imitation of stone. It had 292 glass windows, and the roof inside was painted to look like a bower, with vines and tendrils of fruit.

This banqueting house was much in demand by Elizabeth's successor **James I** as a venue for masque performances. James commissioned a new more substantial building from architect Robert Stickells, but was not pleased with the result. However, his disappointment was shortlived: in January 1619 a worker clearing up after a masque accidentally set fire to the oil-painted scenery, and the building burnt to the ground!

Looking for a far more sumptuous and elegant banqueting house, King James turned to the talented Inigo Jones, already highly regarded at court as Queen Anna's masque designer and architectural advisor. Mindful of the King's previous disappointment, Jones turned to the geometry of ancient Roman, or classical, architecture to design a building that created a sensation.

When it was completed in 1622, the new banqueting house stood out for miles around. In King James's day the building had contrasting layers of honey-coloured and pinkish-brown stone, with only the entablature (above the columns), and the pilasters and balusters in pure white. It was a stunning sight for Londoners used to the medieval layout and warm brick tones of the medieval Whitehall Palace.

James was delighted with his new building, which hosted numerous masques, each more extravagant than the last, and many grand receptions for visiting ambassadors.

The installation, in 1636, of Rubens' masterly paintings, commissioned by **Charles I**, marked the end of the building as a venue for masques, which required brilliant, and highly damaging, illumination from torches and flambeaux.

Almost 40 years to the day after Charles had been executed at the Banqueting House, his grandchildren William of Orange and Mary, elder daughter of deposed James II, were offered the English throne there as joint monarchs **William III & Mary II** in 1689.

A major fire, started by a maid drying laundry, devastated the palace of Whitehall in 1698; the Banqueting House was saved on the express orders of William III. Its south window was hastily blocked up to stop flames reaching the interior and huge efforts were made to stem the oncoming fire. After two terrible days the Banqueting House was the sole survivor of a once-grand palace.

After 1698 the Banqueting House went through a number of transformations, including a phase as a Chapel Royal used by **William IV and Queen Adelaide**, and young **Queen Victoria** attended services at the chapel with her family. The exterior of the Banqueting House we see today is the result of a major renovation between 1829 and 1837 by Sir John Soane, who had the building refaced in Portland Stone. It became a museum under **George VI** until 1962, and then it was reopened by **Queen Elizabeth II** in 1964. as a historic building and events venue.

Charles I 1625-49

Small, shy and stubborn, Charles provoked – or was provoked into – vicious civil war

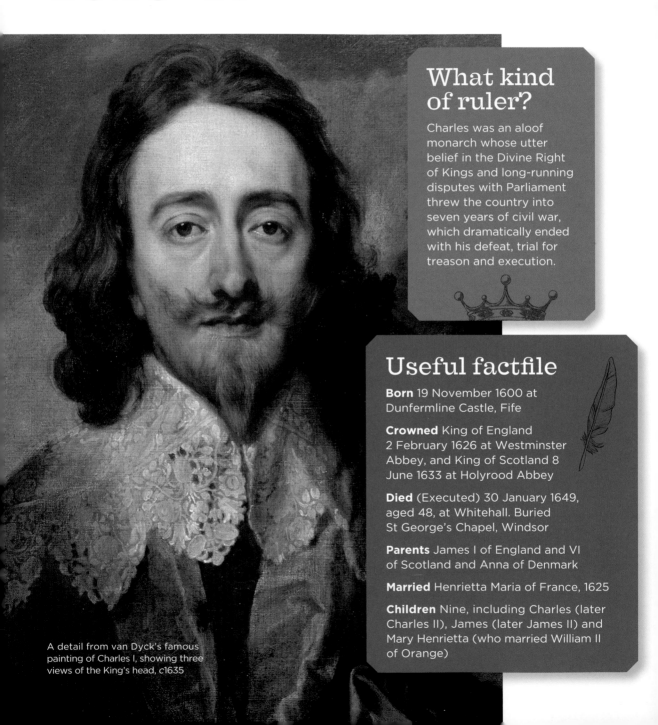

A detail from van Dyck's famous painting of Charles I, showing three views of the King's head, c1635

What kind of ruler?

Charles was an aloof monarch whose utter belief in the Divine Right of Kings and long-running disputes with Parliament threw the country into seven years of civil war, which dramatically ended with his defeat, trial for treason and execution.

Useful factfile

Born 19 November 1600 at Dunfermline Castle, Fife

Crowned King of England 2 February 1626 at Westminster Abbey, and King of Scotland 8 June 1633 at Holyrood Abbey

Died (Executed) 30 January 1649, aged 48, at Whitehall. Buried St George's Chapel, Windsor

Parents James I of England and VI of Scotland and Anna of Denmark

Married Henrietta Maria of France, 1625

Children Nine, including Charles (later Charles II), James (later James II) and Mary Henrietta (who married William II of Orange)

John Weesop's gory representation of the execution of Charles I in 1649

Physical oddity From birth Charles had been small and sickly. Even at the age of three he did not have strength enough to walk and could barely talk. He never grew taller than 1.55m (5'4") and his legs remained bowed.

Most defiant act Raising his royal standard at Nottingham on 24 August 1642 to signal the start of civil war with the forces of Parliament

Finest hour His calm and dignified appearance on the scaffold just before his death. The King wore two shirts to stop him shivering in the January chill, so that people wouldn't think he was afraid.

Worst mistake Charles's dealings with his subjects and above all Parliament were a catalogue of errors but ultimately his biggest mistake was his arrogant assumption that he could manage to rule without Parliament's co-operation.

Artistic achievements Without a doubt the most important and dedicated British royal patron of the arts, Charles not only commissioned work from great contemporary artists and architects such as van Dyck, Rubens and Inigo Jones; he was also responsible for amassing a remarkable collection of Italian masters, much of which was sold during the Commonwealth.

'I go from a corruptible to an incorruptible crown; where no disturbance can be, no disturbance in the world'

Charles I, just before the executioner's axe fell

The Commonwealth 1649-60

After Charles I's execution, Royalist forces were crushed by Parliamentarian Oliver Cromwell, and Charles II escaped to exile abroad. England was declared a Commonwealth. However, in 1655, Cromwell grew impatient with parliamentary debate, and ruled alone as Lord Protector, refusing the title of king. When Cromwell died in 1658 his son Richard inherited his father's position, but quickly resigned much to the relief of Parliament and the Army, who invited Charles II back to rule.

Palace connections

Hampton Court was one of Charles's favourite palaces. He filled it with pictures and beautiful works of art, as well as building its first enclosed royal tennis court and improving the gardens. Towards the end of the civil wars, however, Hampton Court became a prison for Charles, albeit a comfortable one, as he was held there by Parliamentary troops in 1647 for six months, before escaping to the Isle of Wight. Charles I commissioned Rubens to paint the ceiling of the **Banqueting House** in Whitehall Palace, where nearly 20 years later, on 30 January 1649, he stepped out of one its windows on to a specially built scaffold for his own execution. His death is commemorated in a service held at the Banqueting House every year on the anniversary.

The House of Stuart

Charles II
1660-85

A loveable, cynical rogue, very fond of the ladies

Useful factfile

Born 29 May 1630 at St James's Palace, London

Crowned King of Scotland 1 January 1651, Scone, Scotland; King of England 23 April 1661, London

Died 6 February 1685, aged 54, at Whitehall Palace. Buried Westminster Abbey

Parents Charles I and Henrietta Maria of France

Married Catherine of Braganza, 1662

Children No offspring with his wife but at least 16 illegitimate children by eight mistresses, including actress Nell Gwynne

What kind of ruler?

The turbulence of Charles's upbringing, with civil war, the execution of his father and his own exile created a cautious, cynical king who was a skilled political manipulator. His common touch meant that he was generally loved by his subjects despite his obvious Catholic sympathies. A great patron of the arts.

Finest hour During the Great Fire of London in 1666 Charles rode down to the City and personally helped to douse the flames with buckets of water.

Greatest victory His triumphant return to England as king in 1660 after eleven years of joyless Parliamentary rule. He was given an enthusiastic welcome from his subjects and, despite the spectre of his father's behaviour, Parliament placed almost no conditions on his return.

Love life His succession of mistresses ranged from actresses to courtiers' wives. They presented him with a string of illegitimate children and he showered his women with titles, prestige and perquisites. Yet, despite his weakness for other women, his relationship with his childless wife was affectionate and long-lasting.

Likes His had a real passion for the sea and was the first monarch to have a royal yacht. His obsession with horse racing meant that the whole court travelled to Newmarket biennially to watch the races. The King was also fond of vigorous exercise from walking to swimming.

Maybe a myth? During his flight from the disastrous Battle of Worcester in 1651 Charles hid from Parliamentary soldiers in an oak tree near Boscobel House, Staffordshire. Unsurprisingly this romantic tale became a classic piece of English folklore and the King loved narrating it to his confidants and courtiers, such as the writer John Evelyn.

Personal style Highly cynical and wily, not above lying to further his own ends but indulgent especially towards his mistresses and in matters of religion.

Legacy Charles was fascinated by all things scientific and gave the Royal Society (set up to promote the study of science) a royal charter in 1663. In 1682 he founded the Royal Hospital at Chelsea for army pensioners. The first real newspapers appeared during Charles's reign.

John Michael Wright's magnificent portrait of the newly-crowned Charles II

Palace connections

Charles and Catherine spent their honeymoon at **Hampton Court**. Charles also installed his mistress Barbara Villiers, Countess of Castlemaine, and their illegitimate children in the palace. It was also Charles who determined that the ravens at the **Tower of London** should be protected to ensure that the legend (that the kingdom and Tower would fall if the ravens ever left the fortress) should never come true.

James II 1685-8

(deposed, 1688)

Stubborn and headstrong, James's lack of compromise led to the loss of his crown

Useful factfile

Born 14 October 1633 at St James's Palace, London

Crowned 23 April 1685, Westminster Abbey. Deposed December 1688

Died 16 September 1701, aged 67, at St Germain-en-Laye, near Paris. Buried Church of the English Benedictines, Paris

Parents Charles I and Henrietta Maria of France

Married 1 His former mistress Anne Hyde, 1660 (died 1671); 2 Mary of Modena, 1673

Children Eight children by Anne Hyde, including Mary (later Mary II) and Anne (later Queen Anne) and seven children with Mary of Modena including James Francis Edward Stuart (the Old Pretender). James also had at least seven illegitimate children by two mistresses

James II's second wife, Mary of Modena, painted by Willem Wissing c1685

Should be ashamed of Instead of staying to fight and defend his crown, after the invasion of William, Duke of Orange (his son-in-law), James fled from London, throwing his Great Seal (a metal mould used to create an impression in sealing wax, conferring royal approval on important state documents) into the Thames.

Royal scandal In 1688 Mary of Modena gave birth to a son, a Roman Catholic heir to the throne. The King's horrified opponents whipped up the rumour that the baby was in fact an impostor, smuggled into the bed in a warming pan.

Legend As a young prince, James experienced the turmoil and instability of the civil wars first hand, accompanying his father on the battlefield and later being captured by Parliamentary forces. In 1648 he managed to escape from St James's Palace, disguised as a girl, and made his way to his sister's court in The Hague.

Finest hour James achieved his greatest victory as Lord High Admiral defeating the Dutch Navy at Lowestoft in 1665, the first real battle of the Anglo-Dutch War. English fortunes plummeted after this modest success and reached a nadir when the Dutch fleet sailed up the Medway, capturing a fort and ravaging the English fleet in 1667.

Celebrity victim After James's accession in 1685, Charles II's illegitimate son, the Duke of Monmouth, led a Protestant rebellion in the west country that was quickly quashed at the Battle of Sedgemoor. The Duke was executed a mere ten days after his defeat.

Legacy For many years the cause of the deposed King James and his heirs inspired a romantic loyalty, especially in Scotland. This would result in two Jacobite rebellions over the next 50 years, and his descendants would remain pretenders to the Scottish and English thrones until 1807.

A portrait of James by Sir Godfrey Kneller c1684, before he acceded to the throne

What kind of ruler?

More serious than his brother, Charles II, James was an able solider and naval commander. However, his uncompromising Catholicism, cruelty of suppression and obstinate pursuit of absolutist policies resulted in the loss of his kingdoms to his own daughter and son-in-law.

An engraving of the young James playing tennis

Palace connections

In 1681, when controversy raged about James's right to succeed to the throne given his Roman Catholicism, loyal London apprentices came to **Hampton Court Palace** with a petition of 18,000 signatures in support of the then Duke. James II was the last monarch to live at Whitehall Palace before it burnt down in 1698. Mary of Modena's bed, in which she gave birth to James, the Old Pretender, is now displayed at **Kensington Palace**.

William III & Mary II
1689-1702

(William ruled alone
from 1694)

A watercolour
miniature of
Mary when
Princess of
Orange, c1677

Useful factfile

William III

Born 14 November 1650 at
Binnenhof Palace, The Hague,
Holland

Crowned Jointly with Mary on
11 April 1689, Westminster Abbey

Died 8 March 1702, aged 51, at Kensington
Palace. Buried Westminster Abbey

Parents William II, Prince of Orange
and Mary Henrietta, Princess Royal
(sister of Charles II)

Mary II

Born 30 April 1662 at St James's
Palace, London

Died 28 December 1694, aged 32, at
Kensington Palace. Buried Westminster
Abbey

Parents James II and Anne Hyde

Married William and Mary were
married in 1677

Children none

The odd couple William and Mary made an unlikely pair. When they first met, Mary, a 15-year-old striking brunette, nearly 1.83m (6') tall was not impressed by her 27-year-old diminutive 1.67m (5'6"), asthmatic husband-to-be. However, although this was a political match, genuine affection grew between them. When Mary died the King was inconsolable.

Likes Mary started a craze for pugs, knotting and collecting blue and white porcelain, filling her homes with her collections. She enjoyed her life in Holland, picked up the language and learned to ice skate. William preferred to be on the battlefield and was impatient with court life.

Personal styles Mary was the more popular of the two, with a light-hearted, gentle demeanour, keen to do good works. William was seen as very cold, unapproachable and too 'Dutch' for an English king. Neither of them enjoyed the ceremony of the court or approved of the uninhibited English manners!

Greatest sadness Mary was unable to bear children after an early miscarriage caused long-term health problems. It was a constant misery for her.

Royal scandal William had two favourites during his time in England. Arnold van Keppel and Hans William Bentinck, 1st Earl of Portland, were both close and trusted friends to William, Portland having been in the Dutch court since 1664. English courtiers fumed as William kept only his countrymen close, and whispered that there might be more to the relationships than met the eye. William was made unhappy having to justify his friendships.

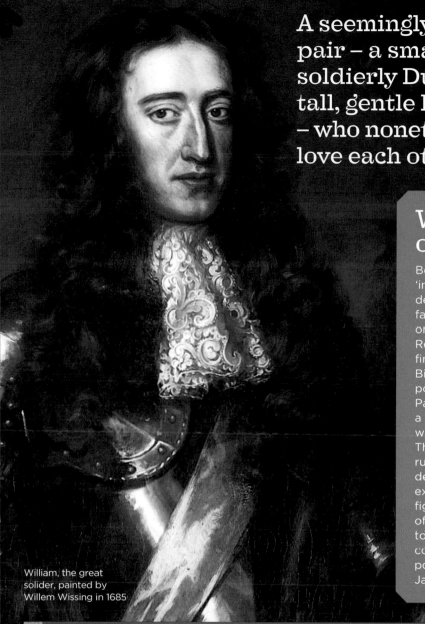

A seemingly mismatched pair – a small asthmatic, soldierly Dutchman and a tall, gentle English brunette – who nonetheless came to love each other

William, the great solider, painted by Willem Wissing in 1685

What kind of rulers?

Both strongly Protestant, 'invited' by Parliament to depose Mary's Catholic father James II. Swept in on a bloodless 'Glorious Revolution', perhaps their finest hour was signing the Bill of Rights, when proper power was given to Parliament. Never would a monarch be able to rule with power unchecked. The first and only couple to rule jointly, although Mary deferred to her husband except when he was abroad fighting. The driving force of the reign was the need to create and maintain a coalition against the vast power of France (where James II had taken refuge).

Palace connections

William and Mary were offered the crown at the **Banqueting House** in 1689. They were the first monarchs to live at **Kensington Palace**, created for them by Sir Christopher Wren by expanding and improving their purchase of 'Kensington House'. Wren also carried out extensive work for the couple at **Hampton Court Palace**, modernising the old Tudor palace to create an elegant baroque front and state apartments on the east side. Mary died of smallpox at Kensington Palace, and lay in state in the Banqueting House, Whitehall. Eight years later, William suffered a bad fall from his horse while riding at Hampton Court Palace, and died of pneumonia a few days later at Kensington Palace.

The South Front of the palace, with the statue of William III presented to Edward VII in 1907

Palace connections:
Kensington Palace

In 1689, a year of Protestant triumph and revolution, new sovereigns **William III & Mary II** selected a modest mansion called Nottingham House to be their home. It lay a few miles from the bustle of London, where the air was clean and fine views could be had all the way into Surrey

Queen Mary II by Willem Wissing, c1686 (detail) and King William III also by Wissing, 1685 (detail)

Sir Christopher Wren drew up plans, but the Queen herself took charge of the project to transform this house into the palace of Kensington, and set to work with excitement and hope.

Sadly, in some ways, the palace is a testimony of a brief and promising life cut short, for Mary, contracting smallpox, died here in 1694 at the age of just 34, before the paint was barely dry.

In his grief, King William finished the building with a grand gallery range which the visitor approaches today, past the statue of him placed there a hundred years ago. His death in 1702 was followed by the short, eventful reign of **Queen Anne**. She flitted from place to place and spent little time at Kensington, but her one extravagant gesture is without a doubt the most beautiful orangery in the world, finished in 1705.

Anne's death at Kensington in 1714 could have spelled the end of the palace, but the new king, **George I** pronounced it very agreeable, so beginning almost half a century of favour and prominence. Under the King's patronage, the palace was adorned and enlarged by the artist and architect William Kent, filled with art and fine furniture and given a refined 18th-century appearance, which many of its grand rooms retain to the present day.

The succession of **George II** and **Queen Caroline** in 1727 invigorated the Court; that essential mechanism of patronage, fashion, manners and society. The royal couple hosted many lavish receptions and led society with sparkle.

The glamour dimmed after the death of Queen Caroline in 1737. The death of the King in his privy closet at Kensington in 1760 spelt the end for Kensington as the epicenter of society. No reigning monarch would sleep within the palace walls for almost 70 years, and for an age the great chambers lay silent and neglected.

The palace came back to life in 1819 with the birth of Princess Alexandrina Victoria (later **Queen Victoria**). The little princess was christened a few days later in the State Apartments, and spent the next 18 years of her life living at the palace. Then early in the morning of June 1837 the young princess was woken early at Kensington to learn that her uncle, King William IV had died, and that she was now queen.

Victoria rarely returned to her childhood home; the palace apartments were let to her daughters. When these elderly Victorian princesses departed, a new generation took centre stage at Kensington. Princess Margaret hosted a miniature court of pop stars and artists in the 1960s; in the 80s Prince Charles had apartments at the palace. Fame and focus descended on the palace in more tragic circumstances with the death of Diana, Princess of Wales in 1997. Few can forget the sea of flowers laid at the South Front of Kensington Palace.

The palace is still home to members of the wider royal family today; they live in a private wing entirely separate to the main palace, which has been dramatically transformed to re-open in 2012.

The House of Stuart

Anne 1702-14

Anne's longest-surviving son William who died aged 11

Useful factfile

Born 6 February 1665 in St James's Palace, London

Crowned 23 April 1702, Westminster Abbey

Died 1 August 1714, age 49, at Kensington Palace. Buried Westminster Abbey

Parents James II and Anne Hyde

Married Prince George of Denmark 1683

Children Pregnant 17 times, Anne gave birth to five babies, all of whom died in infancy. Her son, William, Duke of Gloucester, lived the longest, dying at 11 years old

What kind of ruler?

Despite 17 attempts to produce an heir, Anne, the second daughter of James II, was the last Stuart monarch. Her reign was relatively stable – the most significant event was the passing of the Act of Union, uniting England and Scotland under one Parliament in 1707. However, her personal life was beset by heartbreak and turmoil.

Nasty diseases Numerous miscarriages, gout and excess weight meant that by her mid-thirties, Anne was barely able to walk, resorting to sedan chairs, walking sticks and wheelchairs. She blamed one of her miscarriages on the then-fashionable French dance of Rigaudon, which consisted of little skips and hops. Towards the end of her life she needed a machine to haul her into her state bed.

Virtues Despite her poor health, Anne undertook her duties meticulously. She corresponded with other heads of state by writing letters to them by hand, a task no doubt made difficult by her poor eyesight and the gout in her hands.

Scandal Since childhood, Anne's closest confidante had been Sarah, Duchess of Marlborough. When Anne succeeded to the throne, Sarah became an influential figure in court as she was appointed Keeper of the Privy Purse and Mistress of the Robes, while her husband, Lord Marlborough, led the army. However, the two women's intimate friendship later suffered from a poisonous mix of political and personal differences, culminating in Sarah accusing Anne of having a lesbian relationship with her maid, and failing to support the distraught Queen at the death of Prince George. Sarah was finally dismissed from court in 1711 after three decades of friendship.

Legacy The Act of Union united England and Scotland into a single state and parliament. In October 1707, the Parliament of the United Kingdom sat for the first time.

This stoical queen was either unwell or pregnant or both, for most of her reign

A portrait on enamel of Anne and her husband Prince George of Denmark by Charles Boit, 1706

Palace connections

Anne and George liked **Hampton Court Palace** for its clean, country air, and Anne enjoyed hunting in the palace grounds, following the hounds in a small carriage when she grew too large to ride. The Queen contributed much to the design of the gardens at **Kensington Palace**, and commissioned the elegant Orangery. Its design is attributed to Nicholas Hawksmoor, with later modifications by Sir John Vanbrugh. Both Anne and George died at Kensington Palace.

The House of Hanover
George I 1714-27

George's estranged wife Sophia Dorothea of Celle with their son, the future George II, and daughter Sophie

Useful factfile

Born 28 May 1660, Hanover

Crowned 20 October 1714 at Westminster Abbey

Died 11 June 1727, at Osnabruck, Hanover aged 67, Buried Leineschlöss Church, Hanover

Parents Ernst August of Brunswick-Lüneburg and Sophia of the Palatinate

Married Sophia Dorothea of Celle, 1682. George divorced her in 1694 after she had an affair, and kept her locked up in a castle in Hanover!

Children Two including George (later George II) and possibly three illegitimate children by his mistress

What kind of ruler?

Reluctant. George's mother Sophia, granddaughter of James I was actually next in line for the British throne after Queen Anne failed to produce an heir. However, she died in 1714, six weeks before Anne, making her eldest son George heir to the throne. George wasn't thrilled at the prospect. Britain's first Hanoverian king made his disregard, even contempt, for his new kingdom obvious by frequently spending the summer in his beloved Hanover.

Likes All things military (George I fought in several wars and was made an Imperial Field Marshal in 1707), his mistress Ehrengard Melusine von der Schulenburg (with whom he enjoyed quiet evenings playing cards and making paper cut-outs), the Whigs (the big supporters of the Hanoverian succession) and his native Hanover (much to the annoyance of his British subjects).

Dislikes His wife (see below), his son (a famous Hanoverian trait), Tories (George was thoroughly suspicious of these politicians, especially as many had Jacobite sympathies), England in general.

Worst mistake During his 13-year reign, George spent nearly three years in total in Hanover. His regular trips home and his advancement of Hanoverian interests annoyed his British subjects. It also left the new dynasty vulnerable to Jacobite plots and rebellions, the most successful of which was the uprising of 1715-16.

Finest words Certainly not English! Although he could understand it, George was terribly anxious about pronouncing the words wrongly and so preferred to communicate using Latin and French. However, after his accession to the British throne he signed himself George R, anglicizing his first name and leaving out his second name, Ludwig.

Royal Scandal George's wife highly public indiscretion with a Swedish count led to the dissolving of the marriage and a lifetime of imprisonment for Sophia in the castle of Alden, near Celle. It was rumoured that her lover, Königsmarck, had been murdered and his body hidden beneath the floorboards of the Electoral Palace.

A brusque, shy character, not a fan of court life, or of England in general

First monarch of the House of Hanover, George I in a portrait by Sir Godfrey Kneller, 1714

Palace connections

George I employed the architect Vanbrugh to make a series of improvements at **Hampton Court Palace**, including the creation of a suite of rooms for the Prince (later George II) and Princess of Wales, and the conversion of the Great Hall into a theatre. George I frequently resided at **Kensington Palace** and had the core of the old palace rebuilt to create an impressive series of state rooms, decorated in ostentatious style by rising star, artist William Kent. His fabulous ceiling and wall paintings can still be seen today.

The House of Hanover

George II 1727-60

A good leader in battle. Out of uniform George was dull, self-important and petty

George II painted by an unknown artist, c1740-50

Useful factfile

Born 30 October 1683 at Herrenhausen, Hanover

Crowned 11 October 1727, Westminster Abbey

Died 25 October 1760, age 76, at Kensington Palace. Buried Westminster Abbey

Parents George I and Sophia Dorothea of Celle

Married Caroline of Ansbach, 1705

Children Eight children including Frederick, Prince of Wales who died in 1751 and William Duke of Cumberland, famous for his part in quashing the Jacobite rising of 1745

What kind of ruler?

Brave but boorish. George had an obsessive love of all things military and a terrible relationship with both his father and his son. His long reign nonetheless saw the consolidation of the Hanoverian monarchy and the beginnings of Britain's empire.

Medallion portraits of George II and Queen Caroline by Sir James Thornhill

Likes The army was one of George's true passions; he insisted that his soldiers' regimental records should be sent to him each week so he could pore over the minutiae of military detail. George, however, was no stranger to the battlefield himself, having fought at Oudenarde in 1708 and Dettingen, Bavaria in 1743.

Claim to fame The last British monarch to lead his troops into battle at Dettingen.

Finest hour George kept his cool in the face of the Jacobite uprising in 1745. Even when Bonnie Prince Charlie reached as far south as Derby, George's refusal to panic demonstrated the strength of the Hanoverian monarchy. The subsequent retreat of Stuart forces back to Scotland effectively finished them as a serious rival to the British throne.

Should be ashamed of George II had a terrible relationship with his father. Despite this, or perhaps because of it, George II detested his own eldest son Frederick, perpetuating the cycle of hatred between Hanoverian monarchs and their heirs.

Biggest heartache Despite his many affairs which did upset his wife Caroline, George was heartbroken when she died in 1737, realising too late that he loved her deeply. He swore to her on her death bed that he would never marry again, and stayed true to his word.

Cause of death While enjoying a cup of hot chocolate during his morning trip to the lavatory George II died of a heart attack. His final resting place was far more dignified; he was the last monarch to be buried in Westminster Abbey.

Palace connections

In the first ten years of George II's reign **Kensington Palace** was a glittering centre of court life where courtiers, politicians and fashionable people vied for favour. The death of Queen Caroline in 1737 saw the bright and fashionable crowd gradually replaced by a homely, ageing court in a palace half shut up. Kensington, however, remained one of George's favourite palaces until his death. George and Caroline used **Hampton Court Palace** regularly after their accession in 1727, especially during the summer when the palace would be alive with the flirtations, scheming and bickering of courtiers.

George III 1760-1820

(declared unfit to rule 1811)

Nicknamed 'Farmer George' for his love of farming; more cruelly labelled 'mad'

Useful factfile

Born 24 May, 1738 at Norfolk House, London

Crowned 22 September 1761 at Westminster Abbey

Died 29 January 1820, aged 81, at Windsor Castle. Buried St George's Chapel, Windsor

Parents Frederick, Prince of Wales and Augusta of Saxe-Gotha

Married Charlotte of Mecklenburg-Strelitz, 1761

Children 15 including George (later George IV) and Edward, Duke of Kent, father of Queen Victoria

What kind of ruler?

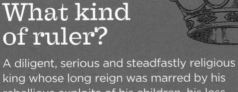

A diligent, serious and steadfastly religious king whose long reign was marred by his rebellious exploits of his children, his loss of the 13 American colonies and his increasing bouts of what was diagnosed as 'madness', but we now think was the metabolic disorder porphyria.

Proudest moment George III was the first truly British Hanoverian; unlike his father, grandfather and great-grandfather, ruling Britain was his main priority and he never even visited his German electorate.

Likes George was fascinated by botany and agriculture. He gave over some of the land at Windsor to farming, hence his nickname 'Farmer George', and wrote pamphlets on farming methods under the pseudonym Ralph Robinson.

Should be ashamed of His draconian attitude to his children. It was well-meant but backfired; his sons, most famously George IV, adopted dissolute and extravagant lifestyles with a string of secret, disastrous marriages and liaisons that left this father of 15 with only two legitimate grandchildren.

Worst mistake Losing the colonies. George's condemnation of his American subjects' resistance to Parliamentary taxation undoubtedly aggravated the circumstances leading to the American War of Independence. For George it was a rebellion; for his American subjects his attitude was unbridled royal tyranny. Had peace been concluded earlier, the colonies might have been saved, but George insisted on fighting until the bitter end.

Artistic/literary achievements A keen music lover, with a passion for the music of Handel, George played the flute and harpsichord. He was an enthusiastic supporter of the newly formed Royal Academy, providing the Academy with financial support and allowing it space in the royal apartments of Somerset House.

Greatest fear The French, who executed their king and queen after the 1789 revolution, and then threatened invasion under Napoleon just as George was experiencing one of his critical bouts of illness. British victories at Trafalgar (1805) and Waterloo (1815) settled the matter.

A happy royal family: George and Charlotte and their six eldest children captured by Johann Zoffany in 1770

'Born and educated in this country, I glory in the name of Briton'

George III

George III as an older man, from an early 19th-century print

Palace connections

George III detested **Kensington**, which reminded him of his grandfather. His preferred palaces included Kew, which incorporated the Dutch House, now known as **Kew Palace**, where some of his large family spent many happy summers. George's early affection for Kew however was overshadowed by his incarceration at the palace during his periods of madness in 1788, 1801 and 1804. The King paid regular visits to the separate building known as the **Royal Kitchens at Kew**, where he took medicinal baths in a side room, to save the servants carrying heavy buckets of water to the main palace.

Palace connections:
Kew Palace

This little jewel of a royal palace – Britain's smallest – began life in 1631 as a rich merchant's house, built by Samuel Fortrey in 1631. He chose to build his fashionable new brick mansion on the site of the home of a former courtier of Elizabeth I, perhaps that of her favourite Robert Dudley

It was **George II** and his wife **Queen Caroline** of Ansbach, with the first large royal family for many years, who were attracted to Kew Palace in 1729. They thought it very suitable as a lodging for their three eldest daughters, Anne, Caroline and Amelia.

The King and Queen continued to use Richmond Lodge (formerly in the old Deer Park at the southern end of Kew Gardens), and their heir, Frederick, Prince of Wales, rebuilt the larger White House opposite the present palace. Poor Frederick never succeeded to the throne, as he died suddenly in 1751 from an infection brought on, some say, by a blow from a cricket ball, a sport he enjoyed playing at Kew.

From 1764, **George III** and **Queen Charlotte** took over Richmond Lodge. Children appeared with great rapidity and were lodged in houses all around Kew. In time, another Prince George (later **George VI**) and his brother Frederick were given Kew Palace until they came of age.

Queen Charlotte added to the gardens in her own quiet way, overseeing the building of a *cottage orné*, complete with a menagerie, which the royal family enjoyed as a picnic retreat.

In 1788 the whole nation was thrown into turmoil as the King was declared 'mad' after the onset of a mysterious illness, which we now think was the metabolic disorder porphyria. The King recovered after a few months, but suffered two more acute attacks in 1801 and 1804. Each time he was moved to Kew Palace away from the public eye.

George deteriorated into blindness and permanent ill health. His last visit to Kew took place in 1806. In 1818, Queen Charlotte was taken seriously ill en route to Windsor Castle and had to stay at Kew for several months. During this time her middle-aged sons the Dukes of Clarence and Kent were both married to German princesses in their mother's presence: the race for an heir that would eventually end with the birth of the future **Queen Victoria**. Charlotte died at Kew on 17 November 1818, lying in state in the Dining Room until being laid to rest at Windsor.

From this time on the palace slept, largely ignored by the royal family. **George IV** considered its demolition; his brother **William IV** planned to double its size but these plans came to nothing. At the end of her long reign, Queen Victoria, George III's granddaughter, opened the palace to the public. After a ten-year restoration project undertaken by Historic Royal Palaces, the transformed palace was officially reopened on 5 May 2006. A few months later, **Queen Elizabeth II** and members of the Royal Family celebrated her 80th birthday with a dinner party in her great great great great grandfather's old dining room.

George III's eldest daughters, Charlotte, Princess Royal, Amelia and Elizabeth, painted by Thomas Gainsborough, 1793-4

George III by Johan Zoffany, 1771 (detail)

Kew Palace, resplendent in its distinctive red limewash, re-opened in 2006 after a ten-year restoration and re-presentation project carried out by Historic Royal Palaces

The House of Hanover
George IV 1820-30

A pleasure-loving dandy, George's king-sized appetite had him bursting out of his fashionable breeches

Useful factfile

Born 12 August 1762 at St James's Palace, London

Crowned 19 July 1821, Westminster Abbey

Died 26 June 1830, aged 67, at St George's Chapel Windsor Buried Windsor Castle

Parents George III and Queen Charlotte

Married 1 (secretly) Maria Anne Fitzherbert (marriage not recognised under British law), 1785; 2 Caroline of Brunswick-Wolfenbüttel, 1795

Children Princess Charlotte, born 1796, died 1817. George also had many illegitimate children from his many affairs

What kind of ruler?

George had little time for boring royal duties, whether as Prince of Wales, Prince Regent from 1811 or later as king. The wayward 'Prinny' had scores of mistresses, ran up huge debts and managed to persuade Parliament to pay them. He could turn on the charm and dignity when needed, but George became the target for satirical cartoonists when his overindulgence transformed him into a gross figure. The 'Regency' period has become synonymous with a whole style of interior design, fashion and dazzling society gatherings, but the ten years of George's actual reign benefited the country little.

Greatest extravagance George's lifestyle was extravagant to say the least but his coronation was staggering by any measure. Attendants' costumes were designed in Elizabethan and Jacobean style, a fabulous new crown was made, set with thousands of diamonds, and the King sweated in the July heat in a gold-embroidered crimson robe, so heavy and long that it took nine pages to carry it. The enormous coronation banquet included turtle soup, veal, pastries, jellies and creams. Parliament footed the bill of around £243,000 for the day.

Royal scandal George's messy romantic life resulted in him committing bigamy. He married the love of his life, Catholic widow Maria Fitzherbert, without royal permission and the recognition of British law. But under pressure to produce a legitimate heir, and to get Parliament to pay his debts, he wed his cousin Caroline, a German princess who was probably mentally ill. Their union began unhappily, as the drunken George passed out on the floor on their wedding night. The couple quickly parted company, as soon as Caroline produced a daughter in 1796. George returned to Maria and failed in his later attempt to divorce Caroline.

Most embarrassing moment His estranged wife Caroline, furious at being excluded from the coronation ceremony, literally banged on the door of Westminster Abbey, demanding to be let in. She was unsuccessful.

Greatest tragedy In 1817 the death in childbirth of his only daughter left George heartbroken, and the wider population grieving too for the popular princess. He was so upset and depressed by her death that he was ill in bed for weeks afterwards.

Legacy The mock-Oriental style Brighton Pavilion, rebuilt by John Nash has to be the most flamboyant architectural legacy of the reign. However, under George IV, Nash's transformation of central London created the elegant cityscape from Regent's Park down Regent's Street to Trafalgar Square that we see today.

The flamboyant George IV in his hot, heavy but absolutely sumptuous coronation robes, painted by Sir Thomas Lawrence in 1821

Palace connections

George IV spent much of his childhood at **Kew Palace**. When his mother Queen Charlotte died there in 1818, George was at her side.

The House of Hanover
William IV 1830-7

Party-loving, womanising Admiral of the Fleet, who sobered up fast when he became heir presumptive

Useful factfile

Born 21 August 1765 at Buckingham House

Crowned 8 September 1831, Westminster Abbey

Died 20 June 1837, aged 71, at Windsor Castle. Buried at St George's Chapel, Windsor

Parents Third son of King George III and Queen Charlotte

Married Princess Adelaide of Saxe-Meiningen in 1818

Children No legitimate children survived infancy. William had ten illegitimate children, the FitzClarences, born between 1794 and 1807, five sons and five daughters

Love life William had a weakness for the ladies. He first fell in love at the age of 16 with a beautiful society girl called Julia, first of many such girlfriends. But in 1790 he met the love of his life, the famous actress Dorothea Jordan, living with her for the next 20 years and fathering ten children who adopted the surname FitzClarence. After their break up William chased much younger women before finally marrying Adelaide, who was over 20 years his junior.

Should be ashamed of Suddenly abandoning Dorothea, his companion of 20 years. William needed to marry into money, and he had probably lost romantic interest in the ageing actress. Although Dorothea received a financial settlement from William, she died alone in France, almost destitute, her health ruined.

Nicknames As a younger son, not expected to succeed, William was not very well educated. He was known as 'Silly Billy', then, later more respectfully as 'The Sailor King'.

Physical oddity William had a strangely pointed head, with a mop of red hair on top, bearing an unfortunate resemblance to a coconut. William found hat wearing a trial (he wore specially made padded caps) but a crown fitted him beautifully!

Finest hour By the late 1830s, William was an elderly man with serious health problems, but remained proudly obstinate to the last. He was determined to stay alive until his niece, Princess Victoria, was 18 so that he could pass the throne directly to her, rather than allow a Regency to happen. He died less than a month after Victoria's birthday in 1837. Benjamin Disraeli wrote at the time 'The King dies like an old lion'.

James Gillray's caricature of 'The Sailor King' in *A True British Tar*, 1795

Palace connections

In July 1818, **Kew Palace** saw a royal double wedding. William, Duke of Clarence, married the 25-year-old Princess Adelaide of Saxe-Meiningen alongside his brother, the Duke of Kent, who married Princess Victoria of Saxe-Coburg.

William IV by an unknown artist, *c*1850 (detail)

What kind of ruler?

As the third son of George III, William had not expected to inherit the throne, but the death of his niece, Princess Charlotte, followed by his brother Frederick put him next in line to rule. During his successful Navy career William was known for his informal manner and raucous lifestyle but in his middle years he became a reformed character; settling into marriage, he gave up swearing, paid off his debts and took his royal duty seriously.

The House of Hanover

Victoria
1837-1901

Small, determined figure who gave her name to an age

Useful factfile

Born 24 May 1819 at Kensington Palace

Crowned 28 June 1838, Westminster Abbey

Died 22 January 1901, aged 82, at Osborne House, Isle of Wight. Buried Frogmore Mausoleum, Windsor, next to her beloved Albert

Parents Prince Edward, Duke of Kent and Strathearn and Princess Victoria of Saxe-Coburg-Saalfeld

Married Prince Albert of Saxe-Coburg-Gotha

Children Victoria Adelaide Mary Louisa, the Princess Royal; Albert Edward, the Prince of Wales (later Edward VII); Alice Maud Mary; Alfred Ernest Albert; Helena Augusta Victoria; Louise Caroline Alberta; Arthur William Patrick Albert; Leopold George Duncan Albert; Beatrice Mary Victoria Feodore

Likes Scottish poetry, the theatre, ballet, music, riding, pets, eating (she was often told off as a child for eating too fast) and sex. Victoria fell madly in love with her cousin Albert on their second meeting and regarded him as the pinnacle of male perfection.

'I was VERY much amused'

From Victoria's diary, 24 May 1833

Greatest sorrows When Albert died from typhoid in 1861 Victoria was devastated, and never fully recovered.

Biggest mistake After Albert's death Victoria shut herself off from the public and much of her acquaintance. While people were sympathetic at first, after two years dissatisfaction was growing with her seclusion. She was persuaded to return to the public eye in 1887 for her Golden Jubilee, although she only ever wore mourning until her death.

Should be ashamed of Suspecting one of her ladies-in-waiting to be pregnant by her hated ex-guardian John Conroy. The gossip was fierce and Lady Flora Hastings was subjected to a humiliating medical examination. Poor Lady Flora's swollen stomach was actually caused by a fatal tumour, and she died soon afterwards.

Physical oddity The diminutive 1.52m (5') tall queen was a slim girl, but by the end of her life her waist measured approximately 125cm (49"), so that she appeared almost spherical.

Queen Victoria in 1859, painted by Franz Xaver Winterhalter (detail)

Palace connections

Victoria was born and raised at **Kensington Palace**. It was also here that she learnt that she was queen, in the early hours of the morning of 20 June 1837.

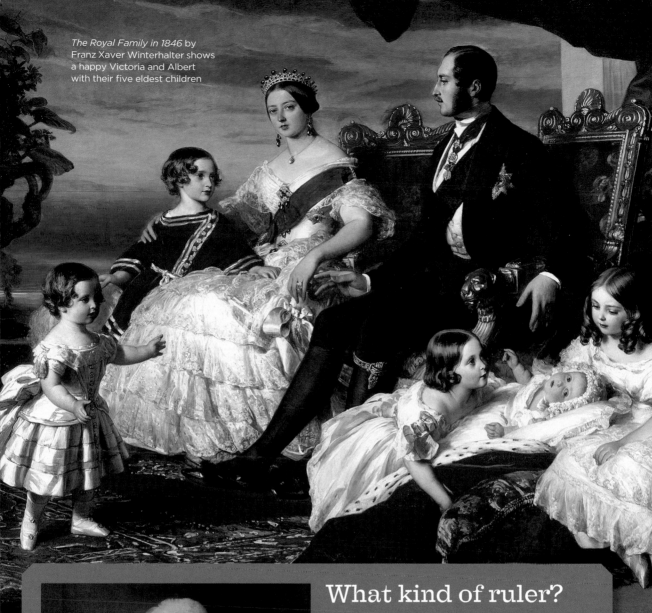

The Royal Family in 1846 by Franz Xaver Winterhalter shows a happy Victoria and Albert with their five eldest children

A candid portrait of the elderly queen, painted by Heinrich von Angeli, 1899 (detail)

What kind of ruler?

As a new queen, Victoria had to cope with the antipathy towards the monarchy caused by the profligacy of her Hanoverian predecessors; she survived three assassination attempts in the first four years of her reign. But with her highly principled husband Albert as support, and with the right ministers in place, Victoria oversaw a quickening in pace of social and cultural reform. She ruled longer than any other British monarch, and in terms of the changes that happened in her lifetime, she could be said to have had the most significant reign so far in British history.

The House of Saxe-Coburg-Gotha
Edward VII
1901-10

The King in coronation robes, painted by Sir Luke Fildes in 1902

Useful factfile

Born 9 November 1841 at Buckingham Palace

Crowned 9 August 1902, Westminster Abbey

Died 6 May 1910, aged 68, at Buckingham Palace. Buried St George's Chapel, Windsor

Parents Queen Victoria and Prince Albert

Married Princess Alexandra of Denmark

Children six including George Frederick Ernest Albert, (later George V)

A playboy prince, Edward had a talent for fashion, scandal and – finally – stateliness

Likes Women, gambling, fashion, shooting, horseracing and yacht racing (the racing yacht Britannia was built for him); fat cigars and his pet fox terrier Caesar, who went everywhere with him.

Inferiority complex As a child Bertie was not brilliant at his schoolwork and compared poorly with his older sister who was the apple of her father's eye.

Should be ashamed of Causing his father's death – at least according to his mother! News of Bertie's misbehaviour with an actress got back to his highly principled parents. An already stressed and run-down Prince Albert took his son for a long walk in the rain and gave him a good talking-to, but succumbed soon after to a fatal bout of typhoid.

Personal style Bertie dressed impeccably at all times and expected those around him to do likewise. He was self-conscious of his ever increasing girth and was known privately as 'Tum Tum' by his friends (who were careful not to repeat it to his face). He was ever the style leader; when his expanding waistline meant he had to leave the bottom button of his waistcoat undone, this new 'casual' look became the height of fashion.

Frivolous claim to fame Society life revolved around Edward, and he was primarily responsible for establishing Monte Carlo as the hottest location for the elite.

Royal scandal As Prince of Wales, Bertie was twice a witness in a court of law – once regarding some cheating during an illegal game of baccarat and once in a divorce case. He had various liaisons with women, including several official mistresses (all married) such as Lillie Langtry and Mrs George Keppel. Tolerant, good natured Queen Alexandra turned a blind eye and the couple remained married for 47 years, one of the longest marriages of any British monarchs.

Entente cordiale Peace with the ancient enemy France was agreed in April, 1904.

What kind of ruler?

Edward, whose full name was Albert Edward but was always known as 'Bertie', had to endure a lengthy apprenticeship under the long-lived Victoria. When he finally ascended the throne aged 60 his coronation was postponed for 6 weeks while he recovered from appendicitis! As Prince of Wales he was given few royal duties, although he performed these well but, excluded from anything of significance, he instead indulged himself as playboy. After a number of affairs and scandals he became a ruler who proved himself more capable than had been expected, with strong humanitarian concerns and playing an active part in European affairs

Edward's wife, the tolerant Queen Alexandra

George V 1910-36

Shy, stamp-collecting second son who rose to the occasion and became a well-loved king

The authoritarian figure of George V with Queen Mary, children, Prince Edward and Princess Mary, painted in 1913 by Sir John Lavery

Personal style Conservative, bluff, authoritarian (particularly with his children) and rigidly punctual, traits all encouraged by George's rigorous naval training.

'Bugger Bognor!'

George V's supposed response to the request that the seaside town be renamed Bognor Regis in honour of the elderly King's recuperative stay.

Likes High on the list of George's passions was stamp collecting. By the time of his death there were over a quarter of a million stamps in the royal collection and in the years before George became king he often devoted three afternoons a week to arranging his collection.

Dislikes George V was a stickler for tradition; he hated modern dress and the wearing of clothing inappropriate for an occasion could easily provoke an angry outburst. On one occasion he wrote an incensed letter to his eldest son who had unwittingly allowed himself to be photographed relaxing on a foreign tour wearing only his swimming trunks.

Finest hour During the First World War George V showed enthusiastic support for his troops and subjects; he made five trips to review troops in France, undertook 450 troop inspections, visited 300 hospitals, personally conferred 50,000 decorations and visited a munitions factory nearly every month.

Royal scandal When the old King was nearing the end, it is claimed that his death was hastened by his doctors in order that the news would be reported in the *Times*, and not the far less prestigious evening papers!

Useful factfile

Born 3 June 1865, Marlborough House, London

Crowned 22 June 1911, Westminster Abbey

Died 20 January 1936, aged 70, at Sandringham. Buried St George's Chapel, Windsor

Parents Edward VII and Alexandra of Denmark

Married Princess Mary of Teck, 1893

Children six including Edward (later Edward VIII), George (later George VI) and Princess Mary

A coronation portrait of George V by Sir Luke Fildes c1911

The royal couple sweltering in the Indian sun at the Delhi Durbar of 1911

What kind of ruler?

George had embarked on a navy career, and only became heir to throne after the unexpected death of his brother Victor Albert. However, his blunt and pragmatic style served the country well during the First World War, the question of Irish home rule and the rise of the Labour party. By his silver jubilee in 1935 he was greeted with a warm display of public affection.

Palace connections

George V ordered that the delicious black grapes from the Great Vine at **Hampton Court Palace** (previously exclusively a royal treat) be sent out to hospitals so that they could be enjoyed by patients. Five years later they were being sold to visitors to the palace, as they still are today. George V's wife, Mary of Teck was born at **Kensington Palace** and took a great interest in opening the palace up to the public, choosing much of the room decoration and exhibits herself.

Edward VIII 1936

(Abdicated, never crowned)

A charming 'people's prince', torn between duty and love for an American divorcée

Useful factfile

Born 23 June 1894 in the White Lodge, Richmond, Surrey

Ascended throne 20 January 1936, abdicated 11 December 1936: a reign of 325 days, the second shortest in English history after Edward V. Edward was immediately given the title Duke of Windsor after abdication

Died 28 May 1972, aged 77, in Paris. Buried Frogmore, Windsor

Parents George V and Queen Mary (Mary of Teck)

Married Mrs Wallis Warfield Simpson in 1937 at Maine-et-Loire, France

Children none

What kind of ruler?

As Prince of Wales, Edward (called David by his family) showed a concern for the plight of the nation's poor and unemployed, at the same time enjoying a glittering, socialite lifestyle. Edward was actively excluded from taking an interesting or meaningful role in political affairs by his disapproving father, instead taking endless international 'goodwill tours', and enjoying many love affairs. He was very drawn to the freedom and informality of the USA, where he met the twice-married Wallis Simpson in 1931.

Personal style Full of charm, emotional, informal and approachable. Edward showed a degree of naivety (some say arrogance) in believing that the twice-divorced Wallis would be accepted in Britain as queen consort. He was also suspected of harbouring Nazi sympathies, and actually met Hitler in 1937, but Edward may have been motivated by a deluded, but well intentioned desire to help avoid war with Germany.

Fashion sense Extremely stylish, from a very early age. Edward is often credited wrongly with inventing styles (the so-called 'Windsor knot', for example) but he adopted or championed trends that emerged, particularly more informal styles.

Royal scandal Edward met the (recently remarried) Mrs Simpson in 1931 and a relationship developed. The couple became inseparable and the American press had a field day, but stories in the British press were suppressed. Edward never found the right time to tell his ailing father. When George V died in 1936, Edward stated he was prepared to do his royal duty, so long as he could marry Mrs Simpson. When it became obvious that this was unacceptable to Parliament and the people, he abdicated in favour of his younger brother.

Famous friends When considering abdication, Edward was supported by stalwarts such as Winston Churchill and Lord Beaverbrook, who were prepared to rally the country behind Edward.

Extravagances The Duke and Duchess lived a high-maintenance, fashionable lifestyle, and spared no expense in furnishing their Paris home. A 1997 auction of their possessions gave a fascinating glimpse into their taste and spending habits: furniture commissioned from designer Janson, prints by Warhol and large quantities of porcelain, silver and glass all carrying their distinctive monogram, an intertwined W and E.

Edward and
American divorcé
Wallis Simpson
photographed by
Cecil Beaton in 1937

'...I have found it impossible to carry the heavy burden of responsibility and to discharge my duties as King as I would wish to do without the help and support of the woman I love'

From Edward's abdication speech to the nation, 11 December 1936

An informal
portrait of the
young Edward
by an unknown
artist, c1910–15

George VI 1936-52

Dutiful younger brother whose quiet personality hid a strong will

George VI and Queen Elizabeth in wartime London, 1940

Likes Stamp collecting, flying airplanes (he was the first member of the Royal Family to learn to fly) and tennis (he and a friend made a brief appearance in the men's doubles at Wimbledon Lawn Tennis Championships in 1926!).

Finest hour The spirit displayed by George VI and his queen during the Second World War became synonymous with the British war effort. After Buckingham Palace took a direct hit the couple lived at Windsor but regularly toured the blitzed East End and other bombed cities across the country; in all they travelled some 52,000 miles by rail during the war.

Greatest extravagance George VI was not an extravagant man but was an obsessive smoker, a passion that did nothing for his delicate health and probably caused the lung cancer which led to his early and sudden death.

Legacy The King initiated the George Cross in 1940 as the highest award for heroism and gallantry shown by civilians. It was first awarded in 1942, to the people of the island of Malta.

Weird claim to fame George VI was a keen embroiderer, having learnt the skill at his mother's knee. On one occasion he embroidered a whole set of chair covers for the Royal Lodge at Windsor.

Useful factfile

Born 14 December 1895 at York Cottage, Sandringham, Norfolk

Crowned 12 May 1937, Westminster Abbey (the arrangements already fixed for his brother simply went ahead with George in his place)

Died 6 February, 1952, aged 56, at Sandringham, Norfolk. Buried St George's Chapel, Windsor

Parents George V and Queen Mary

Married Elizabeth Bowes Lyon, 1923

Children Elizabeth (later Elizabeth II) and Margaret Rose

Palace connections

Kensington Palace was home to Princess Margaret, George's youngest daughter, from her marriage in 1960 to her death in 2002.

George VI painted by Denis Quintin Fildes, *c*1949-52 (detail). Shy George's battle to conquer his stammer was the subject of the Oscar-winning film *The King's Speech*, 2011

What kind of ruler?

A shy and reluctant king, but with hidden determination which helped him overcome his prominent stammer, win the wife of his dreams and cope with the immense pressure of taking on the role of king after the abdication of his brother. George's quiet sense of duty was respected by his subjects and he won the hearts of many with his conduct during the Second World War, playing a great part in re-establishing the popularity of the monarchy.

The King and his family on his coronation day

Elizabeth II 1952-

Elizabeth II has proved to be a resilient and much-respected queen

A no-nonsense and gracious figure with a fondness for corgis and horses

Modern monarchy Throughout her reign the Queen has worked hard to present an image of a monarchy for modern times; her coronation in 1953 was the first to be televised, she did away with formal court presentations in 1958 and launched her own website in 1997.

Likes dogs (corgis and labradors are particular favourites) horses and Scottish country dancing. The Queen has been president of the Royal Scottish Country Dance Society since 1952.

Royal sadness The divorces of three of her children and her sister caused the Queen great sadness, and the very public divorce of her heir, Charles, from his beautiful and popularly adored wife, Diana, Princess of Wales exposed royal private life to an unprecedented level of scrutiny.

Devotion to duty On her 21st birthday, while on tour in South Africa with her parents and sister, the Queen announced in a broadcast, 'I declare before you all that my whole life, whether it be long or short, shall be devoted to your service and the service of our great imperial family to which we all belong'.

Sense of humour On occasion the Queen enjoys throwing off the royal mantle. On one occasion in a tea-shop near Sandringham a woman approached her and exclaimed, 'Excuse me, you look very like the Queen'. The Queen replied drily, 'How very reassuring'.

Useful factfile

Born 21 April 1926, 17 Bruton Street, London

Crowned 2 June 1953, Westminster Abbey

Parents George VI and Elizabeth Bowes-Lyon

Married Prince Phillip, the Duke of Edinburgh, 1947

Children Charles, Prince of Wales, Anne, Princess Royal, Andrew, Duke of York and Edward, Earl of Wessex

What kind of ruler?

Reigning for over half a century Elizabeth II, with her strong sense of duty, has seen the monarchy face an era of immense change from the increased media interest in royal life, the development of the British Commonwealth and the pressures of making the monarchy relevant to the modern world.

Her Majesty Queen Elizabeth II, captured at her coronation with full pomp and glamour by Cecil Beaton in June 1953

Acknowledgements

Published by Historic Royal Palaces
Hampton Court Palace
Surrey
KT8 9AU

© Historic Royal Palaces 2015

ISBN 978-1-873993-21-7

Written by Chris Gidlow, Rhiannon Goddard, Meg Dorman, Alexandra Kim, Riikka Kuttinen, Kent Rawlinson, Jonathan Scott, Jane Spooner, David Souden

Edited by Sarah Kilby

Picture research by Annie Heron

Designed by Brand Remedy

Printed by BKT

 Find us on Facebook: **Historic Royal Palaces**

 Follow us on Twitter @**HRP_palaces**

Watch us on YouTube
www.youtube.com/HistoricRoyalPalaces

Historic Royal Palaces is the charity that looks after:

Tower of London
Hampton Court Palace
Banqueting House
Kensington Palace
Kew Palace
Hillsborough Castle

We help everyone explore the story of how monarchs and people have shaped society, in some of the greatest palaces ever built

We raise all our own funds and depend on the support of our visitors, members, donors, sponsors and volunteers.

Cover illustrations

1 (George I), 2 (Queen Victoria), 4 (Mary II), 5 (William III), 7 (George III), 9 (Henry VI): The Royal Collection © 2011 Her Majesty Queen Elizabeth II (NB Images not to scale); 3 (HM Queen Elizabeth II): Camera Press, London. Photograph by Cecil Beaton; 6 (Henry VIII): National Museums, Liverpool (The Walker); 8 (Queen Anne), 10 (Elizabeth I): National Portrait Gallery, London.

Other illustrations

Abbreviations: b = bottom, l = left, r = right, t = top

Unless otherwise indicated, all illustrations are © Historic Royal Palaces

AKG-Images/Erich Lessing: page 8; Alamy: pages 22, 23; Reproduced by kind permission of His Grace, The Duke of Bedford and the Trustees of the Bedford Estates: page 57; From the Blair Castle Collection, Perthshire: page 60; Bomann-Museum Celle: page 76; Bradford Art Galleries and Museums: pages 4-5; Bridgeman Art Library: pages 7b (British Library, London, UK/© British Library Board), 10 (© Museum of London, UK), 13l (Musee de la Tapisserie, Bayeux, France/With special authorisation of the city of Bayeux), 20t (Centre Historique des Archives Nationales, Paris, France/Giraudon), 31br (British Library, London,UK/© British Library Board), 33 (British Library, London, UK/© British Library Board), 43 (© Lambeth Palace Library, London, UK), 44 (Royal Holloway, University of London), 53b (Thyssen-Bornemisza Collection, Madrid, Spain), 65 (Private Collection), 95r (The Brownlow Collection with the help of the NHMF National Trust Photographic Library/John Hammond); By permission of the British Library: pages 19 (Cott Claudius DII f.72), 20br (Cott Claudius DII f.76), 27r (Cott Vitt A XIII f.6), 28 (Cott Nero D II f.179v), 29l (Cott Vitt A XIII f.6v), 34 (Roy 18E.1 f.175); British Library/Heritage Images: pages 11r, 14, 15, 16, 18, 20bl, 25b, 31tr; © The British Museum: pages 17, 58; Camera Press, London (Photograph by Cecil Beaton): page 99; The Governing Body of Christchurch College, Oxford: page 32b; College of Arms: page 54; Corbis: pages 38, 97b, 98; The Master and Fellows of Corpus Christi College, Cambridge: page 26; Getty Images: pages 29r, 96; The Chapter of Gloucester Cathedral: page 31l; Mary Evans Picture Library: pages 6, 7t; National Museums, Liverpool (The Walker): page 51; National Portrait Gallery, London: pages 2l (detail) 9, 11l, 37, 39, 41, 42, 47, 55, 59, 68, 74, 77, 86; © Pitkin Images: page 36; Rex Features: pages 25t, 46; © By courtesy of Felix Rosenstiel's Widow & Son Ltd, London on behalf of the Estate of Sir John Lavery: page 92; The Royal Collection © 2011 Her Majesty Queen Elizabeth II: pages 2r (detail), 3tl (detail), 3bl (detail), 3tr (detail), 48, 49, 61, 63, 64 (detail), 67, 69l, 69r, 70, 71, 73l (detail), 73r (detail), 75, 78, 81t, 83tl, 83tr, 85, 87, 89t, 89b, 90, 91, 93l, 93l, 97t; Sotheby's Picture Library, London: page 45; © Topham Picturepoint/Topfoto.co.uk: page 93r; © V&A Images/Victoria and Albert Museum, London: pages 40, 95l; Dean and Chapter of Westminster: pages 27l, 35; The Chapter of York: page 32t.

Historic Royal Palaces is a registered charity (no. 1068852)

www.hrp.org.uk